THE
FASHION
SURVIVAL
MANUAL

How to Find It, Fix It

BY JUDITH H. McQUOWN
AND ODILE LAUGIER

Illustrated by Odile Laugier

THE FASHION SURVIVAL MANUAL

Make It, Fake It on a Budget

EVEREST HOUSE
Publishers
New York

Library of Congress Cataloging in Publication Data:

McQuown, Judith H.
 The fashion survival manual.
 Bibliography p. 272
 Includes index
 1. Clothing and dress.   I. Laugier, Odile.   II. Title.
TT507.M385   1981   646'.34   81–3170
ISBN: 0–89696–139–7   AACR2

FOR
ALFRED BESTER
AND
MICHAEL BERENSTAIN
WHO LET US DRAPE THEM

Contents

CONTENTS

Acknowledgments

MANY PEOPLE and organizations were generous with their time, patience, and enthusiasm.

In particular, we would like to thank the American Silk Mills Corporation, Amicale Industries, the National Knitted Outerwear Association, the Mohair Council, and John Underkoffler of Jacques de Loux Knitwear.

Some of the people who helped are Marjolaine Williams and Julie Collier of Christie's East, Katie Kane, Dyan Siegal, Pat Swift of Plus Models, Michele Andrews and Maureen Devlet of Emmanuelle Khanh, Emmanuelle Khanh, Princess S. Galitzine of Jean Muir Ltd., Giorgio Sant 'Angelo, Willi Smith, Jean Bird, and Ann Kirschner of Dover Books.

Among our far-flung friends who shared their most treasured shopping hints, we wish to thank Michael and Antonia McQuown, Chelsea Quinn Yarbro, Annette Lavine, Anne Dyer, Star Helmer, Cynthia Lepow, and Nancy King.

Special thanks are due Kirby and Kay McCauley, who helped so much after our agent's untimely death, to Shirley Goodman of the Fashion Institute of Technology, and to Jerry Gross and Judith Lerner, our editor and art director.

Last but not least, our thanks and love to our families and all our friends, who were always there when we needed them.

The budget is an endangered species.
ANONYMOUS

To buy retail is criminal.
ANONYMOUS

Do You Know?

How to find your best looks?
Your figure's assets and flaws?
What styles look well on you?
What your best colors are,
    and how to choose them?
Your personal style?
Where and how to shop for
    clothes and what to wear
    when you shop?
How to put together a
    knockout wardrobe for
    $15 a week?

WE ARE GOING to show
you how, with a little
time and very little
money, you can put
together your wardrobe
to reflect your *own*
successful look.

THE AUTHORS

Part one

YOUR FASHION IMAGE

1
Dressing Well: Fashion Philosophies and Objectives

To DEVELOP your own fashion image, you must first decide what you want that image to be, and then learn how to make your appearance come as close as possible to that ideal. As soon as you become aware of the impression your clothes make on friends, colleagues, and strangers, you have taken the first step.

All women have clothing problems. We want to dress well without going bankrupt or spending every free hour shopping or sewing. We want our clothes to be well made and to last. We want our clothes to advance us socially and professionally—not to work against us. Some of the saddest words we've ever heard are: "I'd love to promote her, but she dresses like a college girl/housewife/rock star. None of our clients would ever take her seriously, no matter how competent she is."

HOW TO FIND YOUR BEST LOOKS

When you're trying to decide what new styles and silhouettes are right for you, look at yourself objectively in your mirror and pinpoint your figure's assets and flaws. (A full-length triple mirror is ideal for this. If you don't have one of your own, use one in the dressing room of a good department store.) Try taking turns doing this with a picky friend. Do you have very broad shoulders? A tiny waist? A small or large bosom? Are you hippy? Keep in mind the styles you already know look well on you. It's sometimes smarter to have several garments in the same super-flattering style than in many different, but unattractive, styles.

Why not take one day as a shopping day? Wear a good bra, shoes with the heel height you wear most often, and separates—a blouse, shirt, or sweater and a skirt or pants—in neutral colors. Go into a good department store and select half a dozen skirts in different styles: straight, A-line, gathered, dirndl, wrap, pleated, with various degrees of flare. Try them on in front of a triple mirror so that you can look at yourself from all angles. You'll find very quickly that certain styles are much more flattering than others. Use the same technique for discovering which styles in pants, sweaters, blouses, and shirts do the most for you.

For discovering your best colors, try on a number of sweaters and blouses in the same style, but in different colors. Judge color from tops because they're closest to your face. Your best colors will enhance your hair, complexion, or eyes.

Remember that fabric will alter a color's appearance. Very often a color that is too harsh in silk or a similar light-reflecting fabric will be marvelous in cotton, mohair, or wool. And sometimes a color like a pale pink or yellow that is too bland in the softer fabrics will light up your face in silk and other lustrous fabrics. (We'll tell you how to use colors the way designers do later in this chapter.)

YOUR PERSONAL STYLE

Now that you know which lines are most flattering to your figure, you can think about your personal style. Be aware of who you are, what you like, what sort of life you lead, and the time and interest you are willing and able to give to the care and coordination of your wardrobe and accessories. Think about your own personality and life-style to pinpoint the clothes you need for your business and social life that give you maximum pleasure, comfort, wearability, and longevity.

Today, our modern fashion vocabulary includes such concepts as "versatile," "straightforward," "seasonless," "professional," "investment dressing" —all of which relate to the way American women are living and dressing. American women today are defining new goals, setting new standards, speaking out, and being heard and it is necessary for them to create an image that reflects success. (And, for many women we know, their style of dressing has triggered promotions or new job offers.)

Dress plays a very important part in the development of a new image; it is a form of self-expression, something to enjoy, to have fun with. Dress should be a challenge, not a burden. With a little time and a sense of humor, you can enjoy putting your wardrobe together to reflect your own look. There is no longer a single fashion look any more than a single correct hemline length. They both went out in the early 1960s. Women are individuals, and their wardrobes can, and should, reflect their individuality.

It's a shame that so many women have sacrificed their own taste for the "Dress for Success" strategy. This "fashion cloning" compels women to dress themselves in the adult equivalent of parochial-school uniforms, complete with almost identical dark-brown or navy blazers or jackets, pale blouses, and matching or contrasting skirts—and it is boring. While we're at it we should also point out that the more feminine and "grown-up" small-print wrap dress, popularized by Diane von Furstenberg, is an equally unimaginative uniform. Instead of this sort of uniform dressing assuring career success, we wouldn't be a bit surprised if it were interpreted by management as an uninspired, playing-it-safe attitude rather than the intelligent risk-taking approach characteristic of the fast-track personality so necessary for promotion in today's business world.

INVESTMENT DRESSING: QUALITY, NOT QUANTITY

Good clothes are usually very expensive these days. We cannot afford the extravagance and frivolousness of discarding them after just one season—not when a good jacket can cost a week's salary! If we choose carefully and buy quality rather than quantity, we can have a few clothes that make us feel wonderful, rather than a closetful of unwearable fashionable mistakes. Even one touch of quality can enhance a wardrobe: an exquisite belt, a fine silk scarf, a pair of supple leather pants, one piece of good jewelry that becomes your signature. Learn to buy quality because it saves you money in the long run.

Investment dressing doesn't have to be dull—not even with the starkest wardrobe of sweater, blouse, skirt, and pants in black, gray, and white. (The right accessories can quickly update these classics every season.) Here's how you can use color, texture, and details to make even the most basic wardrobe more versatile, just as designers, fashion stylists, and models do.

COLOR

No set rules for color, color coordination, and color harmonizing are dictated by the fashion industry. Designers tend to emphasize one or several colors each season only to establish a fresh new mood; you can choose to adopt the new looks and colors, or to avoid them.

Many top designers create new palettes by dividing colors into categories which balance basic neutral and classic colors with trendy new fashion colors. For the fall, a color palette might look like this:

NEUTRALS: white, ecru, beige, gray, navy, red (yes, red functions as a neutral), black;

CLASSICS: wine, rust, wheat, camel, brown, forest green.

Fashion colors vary according to a designer's personal taste and daring; they can range from a muted, grayed peach to an electric blue. They are created to add spice to neutrals and classics and to coordinate beautifully with them, each color complementing the others. The designer begins with the color scheme, then adds textures and prints to create the foundation of a well-worked-out, easily coordinated collection which is then translated into the season's new silhouettes.

Working with Color

The best touches of color have an element of surprise: the lining of a coat in an unexpected, wonderful shade of purple; the vibrance of a marvelous royal blue suede bag; yellow studded leather gloves; a metallic copper leather shoe. The delight in dressing comes when you can play with your most familiar pieces, mixing them with accessories in unusual colors.

If you build your wardrobe of basic pieces on certain color schemes, you'll have a much easier time expanding, mixing, and matching. Here are some suggestions:

Black/gray/white
Black/beige/white
Black/navy/white—one of Yves
   Saint-Laurent's favorite
   combinations
Black/red/white

Navy/rust/white
Navy/gray/white
Navy/gray/red
Wine/gray/white
Wine/forest green/beige
Brown/beige

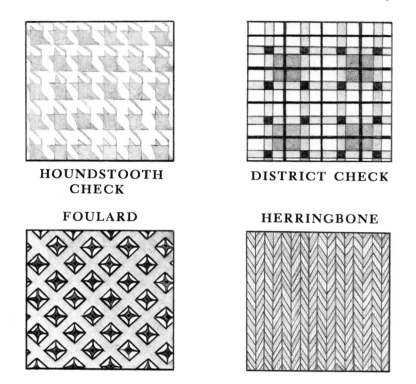

**HOUNDSTOOTH
CHECK**

DISTRICT CHECK

FOULARD

HERRINGBONE

Prints are risky business, unless they can be coordinated easily with your solid-color pieces. Otherwise you'll find, too often, that prints are difficult to incorporate with the other pieces in your wardrobe. Therefore, choose your prints carefully and sparingly. If you buy mostly solid colors, all your clothes will work well together.

Geometrics and woven textures are easier to work with and offer great variety. Above are some easy-to-coordinate suggestions. Shadow plaids (muted tones), heathers, and tweeds work well, too.

As you become more sophisticated about fashion, you may enjoy combining two different prints. This is fun to do occasionally, but it takes a very sure eye and fashion sense to carry it off. If you'd like to experiment, try polka dots or coin dots in the same colors but different sizes, or the same sizes but different colors. Dots and checks in the same colors are fun to play against each other. So are checks and plaids in the same colors but different sizes, or two plaids that differ subtly, but echo each other. As you become more experienced and adventurous, you'll think of many more combinations, based on your wardrobe and your own individual style.

Your Personal Color Sense

It's hard for designers to come up every season with really new colors, even if they've invented a curry-ochre beige or teal blue-green. But there is no limit to your possible variations when you bring all your old color combinations together in new ways. Whether current fashion trends or your personal taste lead you to harmonize subtle—almost monochromatic—combinations, or to deliberately clash and mix vibrants with pastels, you will find that experimenting with colors has a marked impact on your wardrobe and the way you look. After all, the first thing we notice about clothing is its color.

Designers' color techniques can work well for you and your wardrobe. It's all a matter of paring down, deciding on several key colors as the backbone of your wardrobe. Choose the colors that flatter you the most from the neutral and classic groups. Don't be too influenced by the fashion colors; what's popular this season will almost surely be passé next year. Put most of your money into clothes in neutral and classic colors and your all-time favorite colors that you'll be happy with for several years. Pick up a few accessories in the fashion colors if you want to keep your wardrobe up-to-the-minute. It's not mandatory, but inexpensive costume jewelry, hair ornaments, and scarves are one way of putting fashion colors into your wardrobe without breaking your budget. *Shoes in fashion colors are a good idea only if you're hard on shoes and wear them out quickly.* Otherwise you may loathe those expensive magenta suede pumps that were the rage when you bought them last year and are now so dated looking.

An unusual piece of clothing, because of its design, requires a more classic color than a basic piece, which can be enhanced by a more unusual color. It is not easy to pull off an eccentric design coupled with an unusual color; such a powerful look often overwhelms the wearer.

Because of the many variations of a single color, you may find yourself frustrated searching for the right gray blouse to go with your gray skirt. There are so many values and subtle mixtures in all the color families that it's almost impossible to match colors. Our friend Claudia has solved this problem, cut her shopping time in half, and created a unique fashion signature for herself all in one fell swoop. Nearly all of her clothes are black or white. A few separates are red, for accent. Claudia says, "Ever since I've simplified my color schemes, I never have to worry about trying to match clothes. I save loads of time when I shop and when I dress every day." Claudia's dramatic black/white/red color scheme also makes her a standout at work and on social occasions.

Sometimes, instead of trying to match or coordinate colors, it may be easier to choose a complementary color of the same brightness, paleness or smokiness. This will create fewer problems in finding a different color that works with your original piece, and you will spend less frustrating time spent in searching.

There is much more to color than meets the eye. Color is an extremely important factor in your life. It affects everyone with whom you come into contact every day. That's why designers spend countless hours snipping bits of aquas and lavenders of different hues, choosing them carefully to enhance a perfect coral or jade. Color is a vital part of the image that you convey to the world.

TEXTURE

Next to color, the addition of texture in your dressing can create subtle charm and will add visual interest to your appearance. Think of mixing a nubby, handspun knit sweater and a tweed jacket; a Victorian lace and batiste blouse with an English riding jacket; a fluffy angora sweater with suede trousers; a ponyskin jacket over a feathery mohair pullover. All these pieces, with their very different textures, will add excitement to the way you look.

DETAILS

Details have always meant quality, time, and care. In clothing, details mean tedious, laborious, and expensive hours of workmanship spent making a single garment. Think of the work that goes into tucking, pleating, embroidery, or lace appliqués.

Details show to best advantage on blouses and sweaters because they're more visible: closer to your face, which is a focal point, and easily seen even when you're sitting at a desk or a table, whereas a beautifully embroidered skirt might be hidden half the time.

Elegant details, which are a major image-builder, needn't be expensive. We've recently seen beautifully made hand-embroidered and appliquéd silk blouses from the People's Republic of China for as little as $40. As investment dressing, these pieces can't be beat. We think they look most chic when the blouse is white or a subtle color, with the embroidery and appliqués the same color as the blouse.

Details can be even smaller and less expensive and still have that costly look. Think of a black silk or velvet Chanel-style bow in your hair, or an heirloom (thrift shop?) lace handkerchief in your blazer or suit jacket. Both of these should cost less than $5—true elegance at bargain prices!

WHAT THE DESIGNERS SAY

Style and fashion mean different things to every designer. To Jean Muir, "Style is getting it right with seemingly no effort." Giorgio Sant'Angelo agrees: "Style and fashion are a way of life—your own point of view." Willi Smith's approach is similar: "Style is the essence of a woman's existence. It encompasses everything from the way you live, travel, work, and dress in a manner that is comfortable and secure. If you keep your sense of humor intact, you will always be in fashion." To Emmanuelle Khanh, "Fashion is a mirror that reflects life. Intuition and imagination are important. Fashion by computer (which I once tried) does not work because one cannot program feeling, intuition, imagination."

Interestingly, and fortunately for those women with more style than money, none of these designers define a well-dressed woman as someone who buys lots of new clothes every season. They feel that a well-dressed woman should "present herself visually at ease, wearing clothing that reflects her personality, taste, and looks, and should have the knack of being casual and elegant at the same time" (Willi Smith); should "feel pretty and at ease no matter how she's dressed" (Emmanuelle Khanh). To Jean Muir, a well-dressed woman is "someone who wears clothes with flair. She could be coordinated head to foot, or she could add a special ingredient to make her own personal statement. Usually the simpler, the better."

Giorgio Sant'Angelo emphasizes health and physical fitness, a sense of self: "A well-dressed woman takes care of herself, stays in good physical condition. A woman like this does not follow fashion; she knows what suits her and stays with it. She may be a collector and keep clothes for years. Her clothes adorn her body."

To understand and develop her own personal style, Emmanuelle Khanh says that a woman "has to understand her physique and to feel pretty, to work around figure faults and irregularities." Jean Muir feels that "the most important thing is to come to terms with one's own shape and then dress

PAGE 23: *Exquisite embroidery, detailing, and three-dimensional appliqués are the hallmark of Emmanuelle Khanh's elegant, feminine designs.* (PHOTO OVAK, COURTESY EMMANUELLE KHANH)

PAGES 24 AND 25: *Willi Smith's designs are upbeat and exciting, designed for active women of all ages. He says, "People should have fun with their clothes. . . . I always try to give my customer options she can express according to her imagination." Here are some of his fall separates that can be switched around to create many more outfits.* (PHOTOS COURTESY WILLI SMITH)

PAGES 26 AND 27: *Giorgio Sant'-Angelo views the bodysuit as his "signature" garment, shown here in two dramatic versions (rhinestone-and bead-studded) with coordinating skirts. Sant'Angelo comments: "As an artist and sculptor, I see the human body as a perfect creation, like decorating sculpture. The lycra bodysuit is the essence of practicality; with it a woman needs to wear only one garment next to her skin. It supports her body and makes it free and easy."* (PHOTOS COURTESY GIORGIO SANT'ANGELO)

accordingly—not to simply ape fashion trends which might not be flattering." Giorgio Sant'Angelo thinks that a woman should ask herself: "Who am I? Who do I want to be?" He says, "I like people who invent themselves—this is true creativity."

For Willi Smith, "When a woman knows who she is, she can ask herself: 'What image do I want for myself? How can I dress creatively for business without looking like one of the boys? What hair, makeup, and accessories suit me best—not what is dictated by the fashion press? How can I get the most mileage out of a well-balanced wardrobe, adding a few new pieces each season?' "

All of the designers strongly recommended the "pieces" approach for women to integrate this year's fashions (or any year's fashions) into their wardrobes. The designers all stressed a basic separates wardrobe and emphasized the fact that many of their designs from several years ago ("this year's skirt with last year's blouse"—Emmanuelle Khanh) can and should be moved around to create new ensembles. By using this fashion approach of "hold, add, and switch," all the designers agreed that it was fairly easy to put together a beautiful and useful long-term wardrobe on $500 a year, starting with "two of everything" and updating with accessories.

And all of the designers wound up saying the same thing: Fashion is variety. Women should not be afraid to experiment.

WHAT YOU CAN LEARN FROM DESIGNERS

It's fascinating to see how designers develop their style and how they come up with their ideas, some of which have launched their successful careers. For the winter of 1980, Michaele Vollbracht, a well-known fashion illustrator now rapidly winning acclaim as an innovative and extremely creative designer, took a secondhand American Indian blanket and folded it ingeniously to form a jacket. (He didn't want to cut the blanket, which would have destroyed it.) Then Vollbracht appliquéd large colored paillettes (sequins) on certain areas of the blanket's motifs. The results was a unique and beautiful garment, as much art form as it was clothing.

Vollbracht's idea didn't cost much money, which proves that you don't have to spend a fortune, you just need a good idea. With a little imagination and an eye for the potential of unusual fabrics and sources, you, too, can create wonderful ideas and put together striking outfits.

Paloma Picasso, Pablo's daughter and a fine artist and designer in her own right, is now designing jewelry for Tiffany. In a recent interview, Paloma

*Jean Muir's clothing combines the easy grace of classic design with avant-garde fashion.
These jersey culottes from her autumn 1975 collection are up-to-the-minute now—six
years later!* (PHOTO COURTESY JEAN MUIR LTD.)

Picasso stated that she likes massive, boldly colored jewelry. She said that much of her inspiration comes from her own large collection of jewelry, most of which she found at flea markets. These design sources are available to you, too, and you can get ideas from them as you browse.

ONLY FOR THE ADVENTUROUS

As we said earlier, uniform dressing is safe. It's also dull and boring. If you like to feel safe, to melt into the crowd or the furniture, skip this last section and turn to the next chapter. But if, even just once in a while, you like to stand out from the crowd, keep on reading.

We love to escape from the gray or navy suit straitjacket, especially for meetings and important lunches. The easiest way to accomplish this is through color. Why not a suit in a violet tweed basketweave, a periwinkle blue suede, or a smoky green handloomed wool? Or an utterly simple tailored dress in fire-engine red silk or linen? Another alternative is putting separates together into something that resembles a suit, but reveals your imagination and creativity. One of our favorites is very subtle in color. In fact, it's monochromatic, but far from boring because it plays textures against each other. This "suit" is a white cashmere crew neck sweater with cables, a gray and white tweed skirt, and a black velvet shawl-collared jacket, cut like a man's smoking jacket. When we're feeling conservative, we wear it with black or gray pumps. When we're feeling looser, we wear it with gray suede boots, wine suede pumps, or open-toed black suede pumps, rimmed with gold. And when we're feeling outrageous, we wear it with turquoise lizard pumps, just for a bit of color.

Dressing to play against the scene can be done in social as well as business situations. Remember Bette Davis in *Jezebel*? She was a shocker in a red ball gown, when all the other sweet little Southern belles wore white. You needn't go so far, but you might occasionally enjoy wearing a beautifully cut white silk shirt and black trousers to a party where all the other women are wearing fluttery dresses. You'll stand out—but elegantly!

2
Analyzing and Organizing Your Wardrobe

HOW MANY TIMES are we, along with other women, flummoxed because, although our closets are full, we "haven't a thing to wear"? And how many times are all of us surprised to discover in our closets or dressers, garments we don't even remember owning? There is a simple, organized way out of the closet jungle—and it's fun!

Store owners know that an accurate inventory of their merchandise is vital if they are to run their businesses efficiently, and any woman can adapt this principle to her personal wardrobe. With a complete and detailed list of her clothing, a woman will be able to organize her wardrobe, get a complete view of possible combinations of her garments for various occasions, and become more aware of what other garments and accessories she needs to *get maximum mileage out of the clothes she already owns.*

Here's how to start:

For most of us, analyzing and organizing our wardrobe should be a weekend project; after all, it took years for us to accumulate all these clothes in the first place. (Some of ours go back to 1955!) Take a preliminary inventory of your clothes. A large pad will do for this step; later, your final choices can be put in more permanent form in a notebook or on index cards. Be sure to include in your description of each garment what condition it's in and how well it fits. Don't fix anything yet. If you decide to throw it out, you will have wasted your time.

31

This is how a preliminary fall/winter inventory might look. (It belongs to us; we started collecting clothes while we were in high school over twenty years ago, and never threw anything out because we always loved classic clothes. Much later we found out that many ladies on the Best Dressed List also keep their clothes for years.)

CASHMERE SWEATERS

1. White turtleneck—long-sleeved
2. White turtleneck—short-sleeved
3. White cable crew neck
4. White V neck (front and back)
5. Cream halter
6. Beige cable cardigan—short-sleeved
7. Beige crew neck
8. Beige V neck
9. Gray turtleneck
10. Gray cowl neck
11. Gray shirt
12. Black turtleneck
13. Black cashmere/silk turtleneck
14. Black vest
15. Black halter
16 & 17. Black sweater set
18. Black sweetheart neck—¾ sleeve
19. Navy V neck—Sulka
20. Navy crew neck
21. Navy camisole
22. Light-blue turtleneck
23. Light-blue cashmere/silk turtleneck
24. Turquoise cashmere/silk cowl neck
25. Turquoise crew neck
26. Turquoise cable cardigan—Hermès
27. Prussian blue cashmere/silk cowl neck
28. Red turtleneck
29. Red sweater-shirt—Valentino
30. Rose turtleneck
31. Wine V neck

OTHER SWEATERS

TURTLENECKS

1. Red handknit—1955
2. Black—heavy cuffs
3. Smoky blue shetland
4. Natural shetland
5. Gray shetland
6. Blue-green tweed handknit

CARDIGANS

1. Blue tweed cable—handknit
2. Gray handknit—textured
3. Irish fisherman with hat
4. Black and blue tweed mohair —handknit

CREW NECKS

1. Gray rib U neck—Givenchy
2. Navy alpaca—textured
3. Navy merino
4. Rust tweed merino
5. Navy shetland—cable
6. Navy shetland—Fair Isle

V NECKS

1. Lilac—Givenchy
2. Red cotton—Sulka
3. Green-striped shetland
4. Wine-striped cotton
5. Camel alpaca-blend

SILK SHIRTS AND BLOUSES

1. White pleated evening—Sulka
2. White plain with ascot
3. White—plain
4. White open-neck
5. White-on-white pattern with ascot
6. White with navy collar and cuffs—old (wear under navy cashmere or alpaca)
7. White embroidered—Chinese
8. Cream silk blouse—Gloria Sachs
9. Beige
10. Gray
11. Light-blue—plain
12. Light-blue—patterned
13. Red—ascot
14. Jade green
15. Navy
16. Black—Halston
17. Black—ascot
18. Blue/red stripe
19. Gray/black/red stripe
20. Gold/green stripe
21. Red plaid
22. Electric-blue plaid
23. Wine blouse—Fenn Wright & Manson
24. Wine/blue/violet print—Gucci
25. and 26 will make a suit
25. Yellow shirt
26. Red skirt and jacket—yellow trim

OTHER SHIRTS—COTTON, WOOL, BLENDS

1. Red/white check cotton—Sulka
2. Red/white/navy cotton
3. Navy/white cotton check
4. Tan/wine/pink stripe—Sulka
5. Multicolor check—Sulka
6. Rust/turquoise/navy paisley—Liberty
7. Blue/white check Viyella—Jaeger
8. Blue stripe—John Meyer—old (under sweaters only)
9. Yellow-orange plaid—Sulka
10. Yellow plaid wool—Donald Davies
11. Wine/gray check wool—Hardy Amies

SKIRTS

1. Black flannel
2. Black wool knit—A-line
3. Gray flannel
4. Blue/gray plaid flannel
5. Denim—too big (alter?)
6. Wine corduroy—Laura Ashley
7. Green mohair
8. Navy wool—Pringle
9. Camel cashmere
10. Black/camel tweed
11. Green heather—Beene
12. Green/brown plaid kilt
13. Gray/beige plaid pleated
14. Black/turquoise/rose plaid—pleated

LONG SKIRTS

1. Gray flannel
2. Plaid pleated
3. Rust velveteen
4. Green velveteen (take in)
5. Pink cashmere—Bonnie Cashin
6. Dusty-rose cashmere
7. Black cashmere ⎫ also as
⎪ strapless
⎬ evening
8. Red cashmere ⎭ dress

PANTS

1. Black suede
2. Black flannel
3. Black leather jeans
4. Rust suede
5. Gray flannel baggies—Krizia
6. White wool gabardine
7. Avocado leather—Blassport
8. Wine tweed
9. Camel cashmere knit
10. Beige corduroy jeans
11. Turquoise corduroy jeans

DRESSES

1. Rust cashmere/silk cowl neck
2. Camel hair turtleneck
3. Light-blue cashmere turtleneck
4. Wine cashmere turtleneck
5. Red/wine pink plaid—Donald Davies
6. Black/white stripe—Goldworm (virtually unworn —why?)

JACKETS & BLAZERS

1. Black leather
2. Wine suede
3. Black velveteen
4. Green velveteen
5. Gold suede
6. Navy cashmere
7. Rust/white/navy plaid cashmere
8. Beige leather—French
9. Green herringbone
10. Peach Ultrasuede—Halston

Now break these lists into color families by making a card or notebook page for each color and listing all the items in that color. For illustration, here are our color cards for WINE and BLACK/GRAY. They indicate a few more clothes because we didn't include suits, coats, or evening clothes earlier. (We grouped black and gray together because they are really both shades of the same color and combine dramatically for sophisticated ensembles. White deserves its own card because it works so well with so many other colors.)

WINE

SWEATERS

Cashmere V neck
Striped cotton V neck

Rose cashmere turtleneck

BLOUSES AND SHIRTS

Silk blouse—Fenn Wright & Manson
Print silk blouse—Gucci
Tan/wine/pink striped shirt— Sulka

Multicolor check shirt—Sulka
Wine/gray check wool shirt— Hardy Amies

SKIRTS

Corduroy A-line—Laura Ashley

Black/turquoise/rose plaid— pleated

PANTS

Wool tweed

DRESSES

Cashmere sweater-dress

Red/wine/pink shirt dress— Donald Davies

JACKETS

Suede

ACCESSORIES

Suede heels
Brogues—Lobb
Beret

Silk scarves
Gray/beige/wine shadow plaid wool shawl

SEE ALSO

Gray/some Black

Beige

BLACK/GRAY

SWEATERS

BLACK

Cashmere turtleneck
           "   vest
           "   halter
           "   sweetheart neckline
Cashmere/silk turtleneck
Wool—heavy cuffs
and blue tweed mohair cardigan
    —handknit

GRAY

Cashmere turtleneck
           "   cowl neck
           "   shirt
Shetland turtleneck
Rib U neck—Givenchy
Handknit textured cardigan—
    (great as suit-jacket with
    sable boa)

BLOUSES AND SHIRTS

BLACK

Silk knit shirt—Halston
Silk blouse with ascot

GRAY

Silk shirt
Gray/black/red striped silk shirt
Gray/wine check wool shirt—
    Hardy Amies

SKIRTS

BLACK

Flannel
Wool knit—A-line
Black/camel tweed—(alter or
    wear sweater inside)

GRAY

Flannel—(replace as soon as
    possible)
Blue/gray plaid flannel

PANTS

BLACK

Suede
Flannel
Leather jeans
Velvet—part of Halston pant suit

GRAY

Flannel baggies—Krizia

DRESSES AND SUITS

BLACK	GRAY
Black/white stripe—Goldworm Wool bouclé Chanel suit	None

JACKETS

BLACK	GRAY
Velvet—part of Halston pant suit Velveteen blazer—(needs button, lining, but OK to wear) Leather jacket	Cashmere coat—black velvet trim

ACCESSORIES

BLACK	GRAY

Lots of shoes, boots, silk scarves,
two great hats
	So-so heels, suede boots, angora
	    beret, gray/beige/wine
	    shadow-plaid shawl

SEE ALSO

Wine	Rust
Beige	Red
White	Green
Navy	

First a few comments, and then we'll tell you what this time-consuming chore can do for you. Note the duplication of the wine/gray check wool shirt and the gray/beige/wine plaid shawl on both lists. That's to make sure that we remember to use these clothes with both color groups. The black velvet pant suit has been divided into its components to encourage us to "think separates" so as to enjoy it more and get more use out of it. We've noted the designer's name for several reasons: to indicate that the garment is special (it always is, or we wouldn't have bought it, but there are a number of designers we eschew because their garments are sloppily made or their designs are unattractive or unappealing to us); to identify it more easily; and to help us decide whether it would coordinate well with another designer's garment.

We've also noted any special problems the garments may have—such as alterations needed, or whether they're due for replacement—so that we can keep these points in mind when we dress and when we shop. For example, the black/camel tweed skirt that's too big in the waist (the fabric's too heavy to alter easily) and needs a sweater worn inside tells us that we also need a pretty belt; the gray skirt that's due for replacement tells us to be on the lookout for a new one whenever we're shopping for anything.

We also comment on special attributes: the handknit textured cardigan that works beautifully as a suit jacket, especially with a sable boa. Incidentally, to repeat a point often in this book, we never throw anything out, even if it doesn't work initially, or if we get tired of it. We designed and made the cardigan about eight years ago, wore it a few times, but it never looked right to us. So we mothballed it, took it out once a year or so, and put it away again. Then one day a photo in a fashion magazine reminded us of our neglected sweater (more about fashion magazines as sources of your own creative fashion in the next chapter) and we created a "suit" with this sweater as the jacket and several sweater/blouse, skirt/pants combinations.

Now invite your best-dressed friend for the weekend, or as much time as she can spare. Discuss what you consider your favorite look; she will probably have some good ideas on how you can use and expand your wardrobe to get it. Even if her fashion philosophy is different from yours, you can learn from each other by exchanging ideas. Sometimes you're too close to the situation; you've put together the same combinations so many times that you've gotten into a rut. Your friend won't be handicapped by your biases and may come up with some exciting changes.

Turn this into a pampering health-spa weekend with facials, manicures, and hairdo experiments at night. During the day, you're going to work hard on your wardrobe. Put your friend in your most comfortable chair in a well-lighted room (daylight is best) and model everything you own. Listen to her opinions—if you love the way she dresses, you'll usually agree with what she thinks of your clothes.

Outright discards: Anything that no longer fits and can't be altered. Rump-sprung skirts and pants are not worth their cleaning bills and just take up space you need for the things you love. If you're a good Samaritan and give these clothes to charity, you can take a tax deduction with the proper list of the clothes, their value, and a receipt from the organization. Exercise great caution in discarding clothes. It's perfectly all right to save tops or bottoms. (Men have been doing this for years—keeping suit jackets while discarding the worn-out pants.) Sooner or later, these pieces will coordinate with others in your wardrobe to form new outfits.

Swappables: Clothes that are too tight, or too loose, but are otherwise attractive may fit a friend. Why not hold a swap party? They're best with eight or ten women of different sizes and shapes, so that everyone winds up with something. If this reminds you of sorority days, you're right on target!

Long-term-loan swap parties are great for clothes you're temporarily sick of, but might want again next year. In this situation, swapping with one or two friends is the best idea, simply so that you can keep track of where things are.

Salvageables: Some of your favorite clothes may be slightly damaged. *Don't throw them out before you read our chapter on recycling.* You can alter, dye, appliqué, pad, lengthen, shorten what you thought was no longer any good and find yourself with not merely a wearable garment, but one that is unique.

Jessica put the cabled cardigan she knit fifteen years ago (her German Shepherd puppies had chewed up the matching tweed skirt) together with a skirt she had converted from handknit culottes she made ten years ago and came up with a suit so smashingly original that a Fifth Avenue buyer asked for the designer's name. (Of course, Jessica admits, had she waited another year, she never would have converted the culottes because they were the rage again in 1980–81.)

This story has two morals:

1. Don't throw anything out, if it's handmade or unusual. Find storage room somehow, and wait until it comes back into fashion or until you get an idea how to wear it.

2. Work with two or three color families, and everything will harmonize. (You can always add color with accessories.)

Now: why have we spent hours designing this system, why have you spent hours using it and, more important, what will it do for you?

Preparing and analyzing a wardrobe inventory may seem to be an overly time-consuming task, but we have found that, in the long run, it's really a time-saver. It's much faster and easier to run down a list of clothes than to grope through closets, dresser drawers, and cedar chests—especially at 7:00 A.M., when you have a client breakfast at 8:00 A.M. The inventory method has also been a lifesaver for us in planning business trips that require several changes of clothes each day, added to the vagaries of weather in parts unknown. Unless the minimum number of coordinating clothes is chosen, a woman could wind up with a steamer trunk instead of a garment bag that can be carried on and then off a plane and to her destination in town while others on her flight are still crowding around the baggage carousel waiting . . . and waiting. . . . In fact, with a wardrobe inventory, a woman can make preliminary packing decisions before she even opens her closet.

Here's how we did it last October on a week-long trip to London for the London Book Fair and research for magazine articles during the days, and parties, theater, and opera in the evenings. Since this wardrobe worked so well—everything fit into a garment bag, with room left over for a *World Who's Who of Women* and a pair of custom-made boots and trees that had to be hand-carried back, rather than shipped—we plan to keep this as our traveling fall wardrobe for most of the United States and Europe until we're bored with it and want a change of color, line, or mood.

Starting with the color cards for Wine and Black/Gray, we looked for knits because:

> knits pack and travel well—they're crushproof and wrinkleproof;
> knits are comfortable—they "breathe";
> knits are warm for their weight—an advantage in cold, damp London;
> knits can be layered—same advantage;
> knits are attractive;
> knits are very fashionable.

Then we looked for several skirts, sweaters, silk shirts, and jackets or shawls in harmonizing colors and wound up with:

DAY
Black wool bouclé Chanel suit
Black/turquoise/rose plaid pleated skirt
Gray flannel slacks
Wine cashmere sweater-dress
Rose cashmere turtleneck
Gray cashmere turtleneck
White silk blouse with bow
Lilac silk Dior nightshirt—can double as blouse

EVENING
Black velvet Halston pant suit
Black suede Bill Atkinson halter

This added up to:

2 skirts	2 jackets	2 sweaters	1 evening top
1 dress	2 pants	2 silk blouses	

plus the gray/beige/wine shadow-plaid stole and sable boa, a sheared mink-over-cashmere cardigan in case we were in imminent danger of frostbite, several pairs of shoes, bags for day and evening, a black velour Borsalino hat, and a few coordinated silk and wool scarves.

Then we plotted our outfits on paper:

DAY

Black wool bouclé Chanel suit
>   1. Gray cashmere turtleneck
>   2. Rose cashmere turtleneck
>   3. White silk blouse
>   4. Lilac Dior silk blouse

Black wool bouclé skirt with gray/beige/wine plaid shawl with or without sable boa
>   5.– 8. Same tops as above

Black/turquoise/rose skirt with Chanel wool bouclé or black velvet Halston jacket
>   9.–10. Rose cashmere turtleneck
>   11.–12. White silk blouse
>   13.–14. Lilac Dior silk blouse

Wine cashmere sweater dress
>   15. Alone
>   16.–17. with Chanel or Halston jackets
>   18. with gray/beige/wine plaid shawl with or without sable boa

Evening was simpler: the black velvet Halston pant suit with:

1. Black suede Bill Atkinson halter
2. White silk blouse
3. Lilac Dior silk blouse
4. Gray cashmere turtleneck
5. Rose cashmere turtleneck

or, if more casual and/or colder, any of the day outfits.

When all this noodling on paper was completed, we realized that these dozen or so separate pieces could be moved around to make enough outfits for a two- or three-week trip, after which we could always repeat the combinations. There was another bonus, too. Because we worked out the logistics on paper first, our packing took only ten minutes!

This travel-planning technique works just as well for women who don't travel. By doing her groundwork in advance, at home, as we have shown in this chapter, a woman can also eliminate much of the time she spends in stores trying to figure out what she really needs most. Armed with her inventory (ours is a 4″ × 6″ pad), a woman will know immediately whether a tempting new item in a color she's never worn before will coordinate with enough of her clothes to make its purchase a bargain instead of being the start of a whole new ensemble in a new color harmony.

STORAGE

Most women don't have enough storage space for their clothes. We'd love to be able to tell you how to turn a flowerpot into a walk-in closet, but we're not magicians. For most people, storage is a problem today. Many apartments have only one clothes closet. If you're cramped for closet space, you'll have to be more ruthless in discarding clothes, and you'll have to improvise extra clothes space with such devices as cedar chests, storage cubes, trunks, and drawers under captain's beds.

We're still trying to solve storage problems ourselves. There's a trade-off between keeping clothes visible and accessible and keeping them in small spaces, crease-free and sag-free. For example, we converted one built-in closet to six horizontal shelves. It's perfect for our knits—sweaters, skirts, dresses, pants—because laying them flat prevents the stretching that inevitably results from putting them on hangers. Putting our clothes on shelves also let us see color combinations of tops and bottoms at a glance. Unfortunately, though, it's much harder to remove and replace garments from shelves than from hangers. And the pants, skirts, and tops that were not knits became so wrinkled that we were soon forced to hang them in another closet.

Then there's the plastic-bag problem. Plastic bags are transparent and dustproof, but they do terrible things to the clothes they're supposed to be protecting because they attract moisture and heat, which damage fabrics. Cloth garment bags, which can be made easily from old sheets and pillowcases, do "breathe" and will not damage their contents. But they will let in dust along with air, and they are opaque. Unless you develop some kind of identification system for these garment bags, you're going to do a lot of opening and closing of them to find the clothes you want. Stephanie Winston's book, *Getting Organized*, has some good suggestions for solving clothes-storage problems.

It goes without saying—we hope—that clothes should be

aired overnight before they're put away

brushed or spot-cleaned or, if necessary, washed or dry-cleaned when
    they're dirty or stained

hung on padded hangers or, if you're pressed for room, on hangers that
    fit them

mothballed from late spring until fall (hungry moths will eat silk as
    well as wool)

MAINTENANCE

It would take an entire book to tell you how to wash, clean, and protect
all your clothes, but here are a few general rules-of-thumb:

Hand-wash everything you can (wool, silk, linen) in warm or lukewarm
water, with a mild soap like Ivory Snow or Ivory Flakes. (Several knitwear
experts say that Woolite and similar specialty detergents are too harsh.)
Do not wring out the garments! Press the water out gently by rolling them
in towels, then unrolling them and letting them air-dry.

Follow ironing instructions carefully and use press cloths. Be sure the
garments are cool and dry before hanging them back in the closet.

With these few easy rules, you should be able to take care of most of
the clothes in your wardrobe fairly quickly and simply. You shouldn't have
to spend hours slaving over the care of your wardrobe, or go into hock at the
dry cleaners.

LEATHER AND SUEDE

Leather and suede deserve special mention because they are the epitome
of investment dressing: expensive things that you'll want to wear and enjoy
for years.

Those marvelous classic $115 Ferragamo pumps you bought for $28 at
the end of the season will lose their good looks unless you take care of them.
Treat good materials and fine workmanship with respect, and you'll enjoy
your beautiful leather and suede for many years. (Leather, like fine silver,
develops a rich patina as it ages if it is cleaned and polished properly.)

Start new leather shoes off with a thorough *paste* polishing before
wearing them, and *always use paste polish.* Liquid polishes are for little kids
who are always scuffing and scraping their shoes. Paste polish is harder to
use than liquid polish, but much better for your shoes. New boots should be
waterproofed professionally before they're worn, just in case you get caught
in the rain or snow. If it's raining or snowing heavily, wear rubber or synthetic boots; don't ruin good leather or suede. If shoes or boots do become

wet, stuff them with crumpled newspaper and let them dry *far* away from radiators or heat sources which will crack the leather. When they are completely dry, tree them and polish them thoroughly. If your shoes or boots have been stained by salt, prevent damage by washing them *immediately and thoroughly* with white vinegar, diluted with water to half strength.

Suede is more fragile and can't be protected or cleaned by polishing. Use a good Scotchgard or stain-repellent spray, and remove dirt immediately with a suede brush for heavy soil and a soap eraser for minor grime. Crushed and matted nap can be lifted up with the light touch of an emery board.

Shoes and boots will last much longer if you let them rest at least a day between wearings. If your feet aren't in them, trees should be!

Leather and suede jackets, skirts, pants, and handbags should receive similar treatment: stain-resistant spray and cleaning and polishing when necessary. *Never store these garments in plastic—it will destroy them!* Instead, place your leathers and suedes in a *cloth* garment bag, or slit a seam in the top of an old pillowcase and slip it over your clothes.

All this sounds like a lot of work, and it is, at first. But once you get your wardrobe analyzed and organized, you'll save loads of time in

getting dressed every day
shopping for clothes
traveling
storing clothes.

And you'll save lots of money, too.

3
Fashion Magazines, Sources and Accessories: How to Use Them Creatively

MANY FASHIONABLE women with more style than money (or, as British Vogue puts it so wittily, "more dash than cash") keep files of pictures and articles using fashion ideas they find especially eye-catching. Starting with clothes they already have, these women use their file material to create entirely new looks. For example, one friend noticed last summer that many designers were accessorizing their fall and winter coats with hoods that tucked under the collars. She fell in love with this dramatic look and clipped the photos for her files. That fall, she used them as guides to make a "designer" hood from an old wool scarf.

With a little imagination, any woman can pick up ideas for accessories and new clothing combinations from pictures in fashion magazines, from store displays, and from advertisements in many media. Fashion magazines are used most often—especially by those of us who don't draw—because they are permanent (unlike store displays) and are generally in color (unlike newspaper articles and advertisements).

For the novice, fashion magazines can be confusing and overwhelming. Each issue carries a barrage of messages: SWEATERS/FURS/WHITE/ VELVET. Each is supposed to be *the* look of the new season. How are we supposed to manage all this on a clothing budget of $500 to $1,000 a year?

To make matters worse, editorial photographs and runway shots are

45

deceptive. If the photographs were subjected to a truth-in-labeling law, the captions would have to read: "This garment has been pinned, stuffed, padded, pinched, pressed, and accessorized. Its color has been altered by studio lighting." Models are perfectly coiffed, made up, and posed for each photograph. Fashion photos are full of illusion and theatrics. What's left when you subtract the breathtaking model, the precious accessories, and the magnificent location, is the garment which should really be the focus of attention, if that's what the magazine is trying to sell.

Very often a fashion photograph is deliberately blurry, to suggest exciting movement. This is interesting photographically and aesthetically, but certainly does not help us get a feeling for the lines of the design or its suitability for us.

HOW TO LOOK AT A FASHION MAGAZINE

Despite the many disadvantages of fashion photography and illustration, fashion magazines are still a wonderful source of ideas. It's often useful to skim through fashion magazines several times. This way you can concentrate on different aspects of fashion on each run-through and grasp the cumulative fashion message. On the first go-round, just look at the pictures. Don't skip the advertising photos and sketches in the front of the magazine; they show the clothing less artistically, but often in much better detail than the photographs in the editorial section of the magazine. Now, with your hand, mask the heads on the illustrations and photographs. They look different, don't they? Perhaps it was the model's face, makeup, or hairdo that really attracted you. (If the accessories—shoes, boots, jewelry—are overwhelming, cover them with your other hand when you look at the illustrations.)

Now go through the magazine again, looking only at the fashion text, not at the photographs. Keep track of major fashion themes like "deep, blackened colors," "white for winter," "fluffy, feather-light sweaters," "straight, clean lines," "soft touches of lace," "the return of the fur collar," and so on. Just through reading the verbal descriptions, without looking at the photographs, you've started to get a feel for what clothing will look like in the season ahead. Let your mind wander to clothes in your wardrobe that fit some of these descriptions, and jot down some ideas, if you like. Often the vaguest text stimulates the most creative ideas. With a feature titled "The New Opulence," you can really free-associate. Your thoughts might go something like this: "The New Opulence, huh? What do I have that's really luxurious, or that fakes the look? How about that gem-studded black velvet belt from Kashmir that I've had for ten years but hardly ever worn? It could really dress up a white silk shirt and black pants or a skirt. What else can I wear it with? It's really a knockout, and I should take advantage of its being high fashion this season to wear it a lot. How about as a jeweled neckline or as a belt on that black cashmere skirt I wear as a strapless dress?

"And what about that fur collar? That's certainly opulent, and didn't I see something earlier in that issue about the return of the fur collar—especially on sweaters, which are hot fashion this season?" And so you go on, thinking out loud, and jotting down ideas that will pull pieces of your wardrobe together in interesting new ways that are uniquely yours. And so far you haven't spent a dime!

When you come to quotes by designers, pay special attention. Their fashion insights are especially valuable and often hint at the direction that fashion will take a year from now.

Now that you've gotten an overview, you're ready to go through the magazine again, taking a closer look at the drawings and photos that appeal to you. No more covering heads and feet; this is the time to examine how detail makes or breaks a look. Take a few minutes with each picture. What is being done at the neck? Pins? Necklaces? Scarves? How are they tied? Does the scarf add a touch of color to what would otherwise be a monochromatic color scheme? Or is the neck bare, and what effect does that have? Is there any other jewelry? How does the hairdo complete the look?

Move down to the waist. Is it belted? What kind of belt? Wide? Narrow? Smooth? Textured? Where is the belt placed? What does it contribute to the look? If the outfit is a jacket and skirt or pants, how are they proportioned? What kind of line and shape do they have? Slim? Loose? In between? Are the jacket and skirt lines becoming longer or shorter? What kind of shoes and stockings is the model wearing? How do they contribute to the finished look? Soon you'll be able to pick up four or five ideas from a picture almost subliminally, without going through this lengthy fashion catechism.

Next, clip the pictures that appeal to you. Be discriminating; usually there aren't more than a dozen or so in any fashion issue. Make notes on them, if you like. This is your fashion file, a working scrapbook of ideas. For example, last fall we fell in love with an ensemble by Giorgio Armani, an Italian designer whose fabrics and tailoring are magnificent, and whose prices reflect the quality of his work. There was a wool blazer in a big black/camel/white tweed, with matching full-cut white wool trousers ($775), worn with a front-buttoned black cotton-velvet blouse ($230) and accessorized with a high-wrapped white scarf, probably silk, and a geometric lapel pin. Our notes say: "Have trousers. What about navy/rust/white plaid cashmere blazer with a navy cashmere sweater? Try padding out shoulders and buy white silk aviator scarf." Our outlay was something like $25 for a set of shoulder pads and a white silk scarf. And it looked great!

Another clip from our file shows an Anne Klein navy flannel suit set off by a bright red Fortuny-pleated blouse, with bow. There's no price, but the ensemble probably cost around $500. In the margin we noted: "Try navy cashmere suit (from 1978) with red silk ascot shirt, tied in bow, rather than ascot." And a third clip illustrated some of Ralph Lauren's classic separates: a V neck cashmere cardigan, with lace peeking out at the cuffs and a lace collar, worn with a double strand of pearls. From the illustration and the advertising copy, it's impossible to tell whether the lace was attached to the cashmere cardigan, or to the otherwise invisible silk shirt underneath it. Probable price, $300 to $400. And our notes say: "Try with Hermès turquoise cashmere cardigan (picked up on sale, of course, six years ago), lace collar, pearls."

At any time, we may have as many as a hundred clippings in our fashion files—we also have hairdo and makeup files—and we update them periodically, without turning it into a major project. Our goal is simply to copy or adapt designer looks without spending a fortune. You can do this as we do: by keeping a fashion file of attractive pictures which you can use as a guide in switching around the pieces of your wardrobe every season. This, of course, is the philosophy behind investment dressing, or separates dressing: buy a few superb pieces, add to them every year, and keep on moving them around to form different combinations every season.

STARTING YOUR FASHION FILE

If you're just beginning a fashion file, you'll need to familiarize yourself with a number of American and European fashion magazines. Borrow as many as you can from the library until you get a feel for which magazines show the fashions you like the best. (Otherwise, you might spend so much money on European magazines that you'll have no money for buying clothes!) To some extent, your choice of magazines will depend on your age, budget, and life-style. Even if you're not fluent in French or Italian, it's good to borrow magazines like *Marie-Claire*, *Femme Pratique*, *L'Officiel*, *Depeche Mode*, and Italian *Vogue*, Italian *Bazaar*, *Lei* (Italian *Glamour*), and *Linea Italia*, just to look at the pictures and see what the European designers are doing. The magazines we buy and read regularly are *Vogue*, *Bazaar*, *W*, and the French *Marie-Claire* and *Femme Pratique*. To save money, we take turns buying the magazines, and swap them with fashion-loving friends.

Fall is a good time to start your fashion file. Try to pick up as many fashion magazines as you can for one month—say, September. The more variety you have, the more clearly you'll see the many different looks shown for the fall. You'll be able to discriminate more easily because of your exposure to all the looks within a short period of time. After you've looked through the magazines, clip and sort the articles, as described earlier.

After several months, you'll have put together a collection of looks just for you. Many patterns will emerge: you may find, for example, that you're always drawn to one silhouette, or color palette. You'll soon start playing with the pieces of your wardrobe to create your own new look. And soon, with your fashion file, you'll even be able to forecast fashion trends yourself and decide which ones are right for you.

With women being squeezed by inflation on one side and skyrocketing clothing prices on the other, why not invest time and thought, rather than money, to develop your own look each season, by using your fashion file?

While you're inspired, this might be the right time for you to clear out your closet, even if you've already done it recently. Find the clothes that suit you best, that make you feel comfortable, confident, sexy, good-looking, and happy. Paring down your wardrobe will definitely simplify your life. And you'll get maximum mileage from a simple, well-planned wardrobe.

WHICH MAGAZINES ARE BEST FOR YOU?

Let's start with one basic point: if you're a fairly conservative dresser, the American magazines will be enough to keep you on top of your kind of fashion. If you're more fashion conscious and want to be ahead of the game, *W* or *Women's Wear Daily* (*WWD*, in the "rag trade") is a must. And if you're really avant-garde—in your timing, if not in the extremeness of your fashion—you must read (or at least look at) French and Italian magazines, whose fashions are generally a year or two ahead of even *WWD*, the American fashion trade journal. Two quick recent examples: the asymmetric designs which were showing up in Paris and in the French magazines in 1977 became visible in the United States only in the fall of 1979, two years later. Knits, too, were big in Paris three or four years ago. The American fashion industry finally caught on in 1980, proclaiming it "The Year of the Sweater."

Very few fashion trends move from America to Europe. The only ones we can think of are the cowboy look and the active-sportswear look.

One fashion trend that fascinates us occurs all over the world: Most fashion develops on the streets, among the young and poor, who must innovate because they have little money to buy clothes. Designers translate these not-quite-accepted looks into their clothing. The wonderful talent of designers is that they tend to spot these trends many seasons before the public is aware of their strength. You, too, can sharpen your eye for future fashion by watching "street people" and seeing how they put clothes and accessories together.

American Sources

Among the American magazines, we prefer *Vogue* and *Bazaar*, both of which represent high fashion. We always find ourselves clipping *Vogue*'s "View" section, which tends to predict trends before the mass market has adopted them. Despite "View"'s advanced fashion attitude, we find it very comfortable, realistic, and useful—not extreme at all. Both *Vogue* and *Bazaar* have excellent one-page fashion summaries each month which highlight the most important fashion looks and tell readers what to look for in new clothes, and in their own wardrobes.

For younger, less sophisticated and less affluent women, *Mademoiselle* and *Glamour* are very good. Both are "life-style" magazines, rather than exclusively fashion magazines, as *Bazaar* and *Vogue* are. *Glamour* has an older readership than *Mademoiselle* (high school and college to approximately age twenty-five), but there's a lot of overlap.

For fashion professionals, as we mentioned earlier, WWD is a must; W, which is published semimonthly, is more than adequate for serious lovers of fashion who really don't need a daily trade paper.

British Sources

British *Vogue* (semimonthly, unlike American *Vogue*) and *Harper's/Queen* seem to have more style and wit than *Vogue* and *Bazaar*, but their fashions aren't really more avant-garde. Their color reproduction is better because their paper stock is better.

Country Life, a weekly, has only one fashion feature per issue—always with black-and-white photographs, unfortunately. It's a wonderful source of classic fashion—sometimes conservative but never boring, a la Paul Stuart; sometimes more daring, like Claude Montana and Giorgio Armani. It's always in elegant taste.

French and Italian Sources

In France and Italy, fashion and fashion magazines are characterized by a sense of playfulness, wit, and sophistication that we feel is largely lacking in the United States. The message comes across clearly: Life is fun, fashion is fun. *Elle*, a weekly French magazine that is full of spirit and creativity, is a very contemporary, youthful magazine for the young woman who doesn't take herself too seriously. In addition to excellent fashion coverage, *Elle* features a handknit design on the back cover of every issue, and knitting instructions inside the issue.

Marie-Claire is a monthly magazine with a very strong woman's-movement editorial slant. Although *Marie-Claire* often features the same fashions as *Elle*, they're accessorized and modeled in a more sophisticated manner, and the photography is usually more creative.

French *Vogue* is almost like a precious hardcover book. Guy Bourdin's eloquent photographs appear almost monthly, along with many elaborate and sophisticatedly illustrated fashions. Couture designs are often presented in the most exquisite, rich, and creative way. French *Vogue* is much more elegant photographically than its American cousin, which is aimed increasingly toward the active professional woman—an editorial attitude which is reflected in its emphasis on suits and separates dressing.

Mode International's fashions are deliberately provocative and outrageous. Most of the photography is very high-contrast, and the models are made up extravagantly. It's fascinating, but not especially useful, except as inspiration and a point of departure.

Italian *Bazaar*, like French *Vogue*, is an extremely sophisticated magazine. Top photographers like Steve Heitt do several pages every month, and the magazine's visual impact is tremendous. The choices of clothing are wonderful, with a wealth of design ideas much more appropriate for the active modern woman than those in French *Vogue*.

But our all-time European favorite is the French *Femme Pratique*, which publishes the best, most compact almanac of fashion several times a year. Each issue is filled with hundreds of pages of new looks from the most popular new designers. Among those featured recently are Jean-Paul Gauthier, Elizabeth de Senville, Agnes B, Anne-Marie Baretta, Jean-Claude de Luca, Thierry Mugler, Issey Miyake, and Claude Montana. Since French designers present only fall and spring collections (Americans do five: fall, holiday, cruise, spring, and summer), only two issues of *Femme Pratique* are really important. They are an exceptional collection of designers' ideas, and we recommend them enthusiastically.

Many style-conscious women study fashion magazines primarily for their use of accessories. They depend on a few well-chosen accessories to update their basic "core" wardrobe every season. Although their closets may contain only half a dozen skirts, sweaters, and blouses, and one or two jackets and coats, their fresh use of accessories, gleaned from fashion magazines, can add new snap to their wardrobes at very little cost.

ACCESSORIES

Each woman makes her own fashion statement by accessorizing her outfits. Accessories can be your individual trademark if you make them work for you to create a personal look. They can enhance an otherwise drab outfit to make you look sophisticated, romantic, glamorous, or offbeat. It all depends on what you choose and how you wear it.

Accessories are an essential part of your dressing day. They're the quickest way to pull a look together and the easiest way to go from a day to an evening look for an after-work date or party. You can make the switch on a basic white silk shirt and black skirt or pants simply by changing your stockings and business shoes to dazzling metallic socks or stockings and patent-leather evening slippers or sandals and adding an ornamental belt and knockout earrings. Your basic clothes didn't change, but your look certainly did. And your "evening clothes" fit neatly into a corner of your tote or briefcase.

Every woman finds her own way of making her dressing individual, and accessorizing plays a major role in this development of personal style. Don't be afraid to have fun with accessories. Experiment. Try the unexpected. Chanel may have felt a bit uneasy the first time she put on pearls with trousers (which were themselves a daring new vogue), but this little touch of mixing elegant jewelry with what eventually became sportswear revealed something of her spirit and her *joie de vivre*. Now, more than fifty years later, wearing necklaces with pants has become classic accessorizing. You, too, can benefit from other people's innovations as well as your own experiments to create a charming look that expresses your own distinct personality and life-style.

We have a twin philosophy about accessories: they should either be investments—classic and expensive, like pearls, a gold or silver cuff bracelet, a lizard bag, Italian leather boots, a designer silk scarf—or throwaway chic that you won't feel guilty about discarding after a season or two, like five-and-dime plastic jewelry and hair ornaments, patterned pantyhose and socks, and em-

PAGE 53: *Accessories add instant impact; they can be your individual trademark.*
UPPER LEFT: *The big scarf slung over the shoulder accented by ethnic jewelry and an elaborate belt.*
UPPER RIGHT: *Head pieces and hair ornaments lend sparkle to any look.*
LEFT: *The clean classic look: a gold necklace and narrow belt complementing black cashmere gloves.*

broidered Chinese Mary Janes in a rainbow of colors. Accessories at both ends of the price spectrum are true fashion and lend sparkle to basic pieces in your wardrobe. They're the simplest, easiest updates we know.

Accessories for Color Excitement

Use accessories to add delicious little shocks of color in small, easy-to-take doses. It's a lot easier to wear a sunny yellow cashmere muffler than it is to wear an entire dress in such a bright color. In addition, you'll get less tired of the muffler than of the dress; you'll wear it more often; it will never go out of fashion, so you can retire it for several seasons and then revive it again as a completely new accessory, perhaps wrapping or knotting it differently or combining it with another scarf or a pin for a whole new fashion look.

A wonderful, vibrant royal-blue glove, a metallic magenta shoe, a watermelon leather duffle bag complement neutral outfits and help you create an upbeat, interesting style without overwhelming or being psychologically draining, as a much larger garment in a "hot" color can be.

The Ethnic Look in Accessories

Ethnic accessories add instant impact and charm. One of us has an exquisite Moroccan gold and black leather belt; the other has a gem-studded black velvet Kashmir belt, intricately embroidered with gold thread. We've both worn our belts for years. They've created such individual looks that they've solved many accessorizing problems and become our "signature" looks with all-black and black-and-white outfits.

Ethnic accessories—particularly semiprecious jewelry—are very good buys, but we feel that it's best to stick to small ornamental pieces of clothing or large, dramatic jewelry. Large ethnic garments like Moroccan *djellabas* (caftans) or American Indian fringed buckskin shirts and trousers look just too eccentric and costume-y. Only a few women can pull off an entire ethnic look; most women fall into the trap of looking too artsy-craftsy.

JEWELRY

When it comes to jewelry, we feel that it's best to either anticipate fashion or to remain independent of it by setting your own style. Rather than buying the "accessory of the year," like a $500 or $1,000 Barry Kieselstein-Cord belt, or its (not very) cheaper copies, find a look, a style, or a jewelry designer whom you like and start your own collection. For that same $500, depending on your personal style, you could have a jewelry wardrobe consisting of:

CLASSIC ELEGANT

Gold earrings—shrimp or tailored hoops or button style (We've paid as little as $29 for button style with a minuscule diamond in early 1981, but they were on sale.)	$50–$100
Gold chain	$100–$200
Pearl necklace and earrings	$100–$200

ROMANTIC

Pearl necklace and earrings	$100–$200
Cameo (can be worn on blouse or on black velvet ribbon as choker)	$100
One or two pieces of Victorian jewelry (or modern copies) —rings, earrings, or bracelets with garnets, amethysts, turquoise, moonstones, or seed pearls	$200

MODERN

Large Art Deco or stylized silver earrings and cuff bracelet	$200
Ethnic jewelry—e.g., American Indian or African earrings and bracelets, Chinese and Oriental semiprecious necklaces, pendants, and earrings in jade, tiger-eye, coral, turquoise, tourmaline, etc.	$300

Some sources for inspiration and ideas are Elsa Perretti, Angela Cummings, and Paloma Picasso, who design jewelry for Tiffany; museum collections from many countries and eras; and even good modern copies like Monet and Trifari.

We've been struck by the fact that we've been able to buy genuine antique Greek and Roman jewelry (300 B.C. to 300 A.D.) for $100 to $400—and that's for pure gold! (Ancient jewelers didn't know how to alloy gold down to 14K or 18K, so it's all 24K.) We've also bought antique ivory figurines, which we converted to pendants, for less than $100. At the same time, we've bought outrageous junk jewelry for 25 cents to $2.00.

We insist on only one criterion, and think you should, too: All jewelry—and, in fact, all accessories—should make a statement and should enhance the outfits they're worn with. If you sheepishly follow fashion trends, you'll be overwhelmed by the quantity of baubles and beads that you'll accumulate which will date themselves all too soon.

SHOES

Shoes are an investment today. It's almost impossible to find a decent pair for less than $60 or $70. Either buy classics that will look as attractive and stylish a year from now as they do today, or buy a shoe that is so eccentric that it makes a statement of style that is dateless because it is so powerful. If you try to compromise and play it safe by taking the middle of the road, your shoes will be out of fashion almost before you get a chance to enjoy them.

Because few of us can afford to collect shoes or to discard them after just one season, it's a good idea to sit down and analyze your needs and your individual style before you shop for shoes. Many women we know save money by buying "investment" shoes for their fall and winter wardrobes and inexpensive brightly colored leather sandals and cloth and canvas espadrilles and slings for their more lighthearted, more laundered, and more discardable spring and summer wardrobes.

Just as the choice of your basic wardrobe does, accessories require calculated decisions—especially when you are coordinating and creating your own fashion statement. Have fun with these added easy pieces, and you'll put together a charming, totally individual look.

Part two

FABRIC
AND
TAILORING

4
All About Fabric

For ANYONE who loves clothing, fabric is extremely important. The way a fabric feels to the touch (its "hand") and the way it falls (its "drape") often reveal its true character. But modern technology can sometimes fool us. Because of the wide range of weaving techniques and finishing processes, which drastically alter the look of fibers, what you thought was leather may be a highly polished cotton chintz. And what you thought was silk may be high-quality polyester.

Fabric is the backbone of a garment. While it's not important for women to be fabric experts (after all, in how many fields are we supposed to be experts?), it's certainly useful to know some basic characteristics about fabric that determine the life of a garment, its durability, and its care. Some of these characteristics can be determined from the garment's label. Others are obvious to anyone who looks at or touches the garment.

1. *Fiber content*—the principal factor in determining the comfort, care, handling, and life of the garment.

2. *Luster*—Does the fabric have a shiny, iridescent appearance? Does it reflect light from its surface?

3. *Shape retention*—Will the fabric return to its original shape after it is stretched?

4. *Drapability*—How does the fabric fall?

5. *Heat retention*—Does the fabric retain or release body heat? This characteristic and the next one—breathability—determine the fabric's trans-

seasonal usefulness. (Trans-seasonal fabrics add lots of mileage to your clothing dollar.)

6. *Breathability*—Does the fabric's weave allow air to circulate and absorb moisture? These are key factors that determine comfort and are especially important to women who live in humid climates.

7. *Affinity for dyes*—This factor depends primarily on the extent to which the fabric is breathable and absorbs water (including the dye particles). Natural fibers—cotton, linen, silk, and wool—have high breathability and take dyes very well. Synthetics like polyester have low breathability and do not dye well.

8. *Shrinkage control*—What finish has been applied to the fabric to minimize shrinkage? *Sanforized* (guaranteed less than 1% shrinkage) is more desirable than *pre-shrunk* (less than 3% shrinkage).

9. *Flammability*—Can the fabric ignite and burn? This is an important safety factor for sleepwear.

10. *Creasability*—Will the fabric wrinkle a lot? To check it, bunch some in your fist and release.

11. *Pilling*—Does the fabric ball up on the surface? Polyester is notorious for pilling. Wool can pill, too.

12. *Wash-and-wear*—Will the garment require little or no ironing?

13. *Pressing*—Will heat discolor, melt, or burn the fabric?

14. *Surface texture*—What sort of "hand" does the fabric have? Crisp? Soft? Lustrously silky? Harsh? Rough? Hairy?

Now let's explore the wide range of fabrics and their fiber characteristics so that you can determine their advantages, disadvantages, and suitability for particular climates, seasons, and life-styles. Each fabric is accompanied by a handy chart to help you decide on its suitability for you.

WOOL

Wool is the oldest fiber known to man, and the most versatile. Bedouins wear it in the desert heat, and Jacques Cousteau and his crew wear it in Antarctica. Depending on its weight, wool can be as sheer as cotton or as thick as a heavy loden cloth. Wool is a protein fiber and is extremely fire-resistant. It is comfortable in humid weather because it absorbs moisture without becoming wet and clammy. Its springy elasticity helps the body retain its warmth.

Wool's felting (shrinkage) is unique and distinguishes it from every other fiber. While it has advantages in making certain types of dense wool fabric, it's also a reminder to anyone who has ever washed a wool sweater carelessly and wound up with an unrecognizable clump of wool. Wools should be washed by hand (instructions follow) or dry-cleaned. Wools do not soil easily, and dirt removal is rarely a problem. Grease and oil spots do not stain wool as easily as they do other fibers.

Wools—both wovens and knits—need to rest between wearings in order to spring back to their original shape. You can speed their recovery by hanging woolens in a hot, steamy bathroom.

Clothing manufacturers today are combining wool with man-made fibers to give the appearance of wool with easier care and lower price. If the blends are done well, with wool predominating (at least 80%), the luxury "hand" and "drape" will be retained, and durability and wrinkle resistance will be increased.

Wool and many other fine fabrics take a beating at the dry cleaners. Wash them by hand whenever possible, using the directions below, and your beautiful garments will last as long as you do.

Hand-washing Instructions

1. Fill a basin with lukewarm water and add a mild soap like castile, Ivory Snow, or Lux. The hand-wash cycle of washing machines is too harsh. So, as we've already said, is Woolite, according to many knitwear specialists.

2. Dissolve the soap completely. Then immerse the garment and let it soak for a while. Knead the fabric gently to remove any embedded dirt. *Do not pull or stretch*—fabrics lose their strength when they're wet.

3. Rinse in lukewarm water several times until the water remains clear, indicating that all the soap has been removed. Soap residue will flatten and dry the sweater and make it feel greasy.

4. Gently squeeze garments to remove excess water. *Do not twist, wring, or stretch.*

5. Hanging wet garments makes them stretch out of shape. Instead place them on a terrycloth towel, roll them up like a jelly roll, and then unroll them and let them dry, turning them every four or five hours. Or lay a window screen across your bathtub or sink, put the terrycloth towels on it, and place the garments on top of the towels to block them. *Keep them away from direct sunlight and heat.*

6. When the garment is almost dry but still damp, it can be ironed or left to dry naturally. Use a dry iron. Steam irons can deposit rust on fabric and stain it.

7. For a more lofty (fluffy) look, sweater-knits can be thrown into the dryer for 2 to 3 minutes at the *lowest* heat setting.

	FABRIC	DESCRIPTION	DRAPABILITY	CREASE RESISTANCE	FRICTION RESISTANCE
WEAVES	*Crêpe*	This fabric comes in a variety of weights. It is usually woven with highly twisted yarns, creating a springy fabric with a crinkled pebbly surface.	Good	Fair to Good	Good
	Flannel	A lightweight, loosely woven fabric. Sometimes fibers are brushed, creating a napped surface.	Fair	Good	Good
	Gabardine	A lengthwise faced steep diagonal twill weave with very fine but prominent wales, used most often for coats and suits.	Fair to Bad	Good	Good
	Twill	A fabric woven with parallel diagonal lines or ribs.	Fair	Good	Good
	Velour	A fabric with a pile like velvet and a thick, plushy surface which is soft and rich.	Fair	Good	The pile surface of the fabric is not as fragile as that of velvet, but it still can be crushed. Friction can wear away surface fibers.
WOOL FAMILY	*Alpaca, Llama Hair*	Thick, lustrous, and strong fibers with a weightless quality.	Fair to Good	Good	This fiber can lose its furry quality in friction areas. Fair
	Angora	Extremely soft, slippery, hairy fiber with a wonderfully fluffy, furry texture. Usually blended with other fibers because of price and shedding hairs.	Excellent. Soft and pliable fiber	Excellent	" To keep hair from shedding, refrigerate your garment before wearing.
	Angora and Wool Blend	Angora is often blended with other natural and synthetic fibers for increased durability and moderate prices. Wool and angora is not as fluffy, but is more durable.	Good	Good to Excellent	"
	Camel's Hair	Soft, durable fiber used mostly in suiting fabric and not in knits.	Fair to Bad	Good	Good
	Cashmere	A light, airy, lustrous, soft, comfortable luxury fabric and fiber which is warm and extremely lightweight.	Good. Soft and pliable	Good	Cashmere will "pill" (develop small balls on the surface of the fabric). A natural result of friction, these balls are removable with a lint brush.

BREATHABILITY	WASHING INSTRUCTIONS	IRONING INSTRUCTIONS
Good	Dry-clean only.	Dry iron on the wrong side is advised. Use a press cloth so as not to flatten the pebbly texture. Do not overpress.
Good	Dry-clean only.	"
Good	Because of this fabric's distinct diagonal texture, it tends not to show dirt or soiling as rapidly as a flat-surfaced fabric. Dry-clean only.	" Press lightly so as not to flatten the diagonal-rib texture.
Good	"	"
Good	Dry-clean only.	Dry iron on the wrong side is advised. You may want to pad your ironing board and use a press cloth to protect surface fibers from crushing.
Good	Hand-wash light-colored solids. Dark and bright colors should be dry-cleaned as these colors may bleed or run.	Steam this fabric very carefully with a clean iron on the wrong side. Do not touch the garment with the iron as these fibers scorch easily.
Excellent	Dry-clean only.	" Steam minimally.
"	"	"
Said to have the best insulation properties of any of the wool fibers. Excellent	"	Because this fabric often has a nap, it should be ironed on the wrong side using a press cloth.
High insulating value. Excellent	Dry-clean or follow hand-washing instructions we have included in this chapter. We suggest wetting an area first to see if it is colorfast.	Cashmere fabrics often have a nap. They should be pressed on the wrong side using a press cloth. Cashmere knits should be steamed, but the iron should never touch the fiber.

FABRIC	DESCRIPTION	DRAPABILITY	CREASE RESISTANCE	FRICTION RESISTANCE
Cashmere and Silk Blend	Light- to heavyweight fabric with a springy hand and the lustrous sheen of silk combined with the extremely soft and pliable properties of cashmere, creating a dressier comfortable fabric.	Good. Soft and pliable	Good	Cashmere will "pill" (develop small balls on the surface of the fabric). A natural result of friction, these balls are removable with a lint brush.
Cashmere and Wool Blend	Heavier than 100% cashmere and not as soft or light, this moderately priced blend offers the luxury of cashmere at an affordable price.	Good to Fair	"	More durable than 100% cashmere.
Lambswool	Finer and softer than wool from sheep, this wool is the first shearing.	Fair	Good	Good
Mohair	Lustrous, long, and strong fiber somewhat coarser than wool. This fiber is characterized by its lightweight, lofty, silklike luster.	Very resilient fiber. Good	Good	Has terrific insulating properties providing weightless warmth. Good
Mohair and Wool Blend	Mohair adds a fine sheen to the softness of wool along with its hairy quality. Mohair is reportedly 3 times stronger than wool.	Good	Good	Good
Silk and Wool Blend	Light- to heavyweight fabric with a springy hand and a low lustrous sheen that 100% wool does not have. Great insulating qualities.	Good	Good	Good
Shetland	A springy medium-textured wool with a bloomy, lofty surface.	Fair	Fair	Good
Wool and Acrylic	This blend is often hard to distinguish from 100% wool. This combination produces a washable, shrink-resistant fabric at a moderate price.	Fair	Good to Excellent	Good to Excellent
Wool Knits	All wool fibers have superb shape-keeping properties when knitted.	Depends upon weight and fiber.	Excellent	Good

WOOL BLENDS

BREATHABILITY	WASHING INSTRUCTIONS	IRONING INSTRUCTIONS
High insulating value. Excellent	Dry-clean or follow hand-washing instructions we have included in this chapter. We suggest wetting an area first to see if it is colorfast.	Cashmere fabrics often have a nap. They should be pressed on the wrong side using a press cloth. Cashmere knits should be steamed, but the iron should never touch the fiber.
"	"	"
Good	Lambswool shrinks more readily than any other wool. This felting makes laundering a problem, so we advise dry-cleaning.	Steam this fabric very carefully with a clean iron on the wrong side. Do not touch the garment with iron without using a press cloth.
Good	Mohair has more resistance to dust than wool. 100% mohair does not shrink, so it can be easily and safely washed. Test a small area first. Good affinity for dyes.	"
Good	Mohair strengthens the wool, creating an extremely durable blend that is hand-washable.	"
Good	Light-colored solids can be hand-washed but must be handled with care as both fibers lose a lot of strength when wet.	Use warm dry iron on a damp garment on the wrong side.
Good	This fiber becomes extremely soft and lofty when hand-washed and tumble-dried. This fiber shrinks, so we advise following instructions on garment.	Steam this fabric carefully with a clean iron on the wrong side as with lambswool.
Fair	Hand- and machine-washable.	"
Depends upon fiber content	Refer to above chart for washing instructions, depending upon fiber content.	Wool knits should be blocked to desired size, then steamed with a clean iron on the wrong side. They should remain blocked for several hours to recover and relax after washing and steaming.

SILK

Silk has always been synonymous with quality and luxury. Is there a woman alive who hasn't desired a closetful of silk blouses, who hasn't lusted after silk lingerie? Silk's lustrous sheen and softness are flattering to the complexion and caress the skin. Silk is practical, too. Because of its wonderful insulating properties, winter campers, skiers, and explorers wear silk socks under woolen ones to keep their feet warm and dry and silk ski masks to protect their faces and necks from windburn and frostbite.

Silk is not as elastic as wool, and all-silk sweaters lack the resilience of silk blends. To improve silk's elasticity and recovery, knitwear designers often use luxury blends of 60% cashmere/40% silk or 60% lambswool or merino/40% silk.

Although silk is strong, it is also very fragile and should be treated with care. Silk is very susceptible to prolonged sunlight, which yellows and damages whites and pastel colors, and fades bright and dark colors. Perspiration and deodorant stains are frustrating (deodorants can stain worse than perspiration), but can be reduced or avoided by wearing blouses and shirts one size larger than usual, so that they hang away from the underarms; or by wearing lightweight dress shields.

SILK AND

FABRIC	DESCRIPTION	DRAPABILITY	CREASE RESISTANCE	FRICTION RESISTANCE
Broadcloth	A fine, smooth medium- to lightweight plain silk cloth with a soft, stable hand and a low luster.	Depends upon weight. Fair	Fair	Good
Brocade	A very rich fabric with a raised design woven in, often with velvet or metallic threads. These fabrics are reversible and usually multicolored.	Fair to Bad	Fair	Extremely fragile fabric. Excessive friction will cause metal threads to wear away, destroying life and look of garment.
Cashmere and Silk Blend	Light- to heavyweight fabric with a springy hand combining the soft lofty character with the lustrous sheen of silk for a dressier look.	Good	Good	Good
Charmeuse	A very fine lightweight, soft, satin-faced silk crêpe with a lustrous smooth surface.	Excellent	Fair	Good

Because of silk's new popularity, fabric manufacturers have brought out an exquisite assortment of different silks—either pure, or blended with other natural fibers, or with man-made fibers.

Silk Blends

Although we prefer natural fibers and natural-fiber blends, manufacturers often combine silk with synthetic fibers to increase washability and crease resistance. Jack Mulqueen's "Silksational" is one such blend, offering better crease resistance than pure silk, at about half the price. All silk/synthetic blends, except those with rayon, are more heat sensitive and have less breathability than pure silk or silk/natural blends.

Care

Bright and dark silks should be dry-cleaned because they are more likely to run or discolor when they are washed. Silk clothing with embroidery, appliqués, beading, pleating, or bound or covered buttons, should be dry-cleaned because hand-washing can hurt the garment's details.

Crêpe de chine, silk linen, broadcloth, and similar silk fabrics (see chart) can be hand-washed with care, following the instructions for wool knits earlier

ILK BLENDS

BREATHABILITY	WASHING INSTRUCTIONS	IRONING INSTRUCTIONS
Good	Light-colored solids are hand-washable. Multicolored, dark, or bright colors should be dry-cleaned.	Dampen garment and dry-iron at the silk setting on wrong side of garment.
Fair	Dry-clean only.	When pressing a raised brocade, pad your ironing board with a towel so that you don't flatten the fabric. Use a press cloth on the wrong side of garment. Test the effect of heat on a small sample as some metallics melt.
Good	Light-colored solids are hand-washable. Dark, bright, or printed fabrics should be dry-cleaned.	Dampen garment and dry-iron at the silk setting on wrong side of the garment.
Good	Dry-clean only.	Dry-iron on wrong side as dampening or steam may cause spotting. Use press cloth to prevent flattening of the crêpe back. Steam may cause permanent puckering or dulling of fibers.

FABRIC	DESCRIPTION	DRAPABILITY	CREASE RESISTANCE	FRICTION RESISTANCE
Chiffon	A thin, weightless, fluttery, sheer and transparent cloth in a plain, flat silk weave. Used most frequently for evening wear.	Filmy, soft, sheer fabric. Good	Fair	Good
Cotton and Silk Blend	A springy, wrinkle-resistant blend which resembles 100% cotton, with a low luster.	Good	Fair	Good
Crêpe	This fabric comes in a variety of weights. It is usually woven with highly twisted yarns, creating a springy fabric with a crinkled pebbly surface.	Excellent	Good	Good
Gauze	A variety of sheer to heavy silks with an open weave, usually thin, light, and transparent.	Good	Fair	Good
Lamé	A blend of silk and metallic gold or silver threads which are interwoven. A supremely elegant, dressy fabric.	Good	Fair	Friction can wear away metal threads. It is best not to fold these garments too much. Fair
Moiré	Classified as a type of taffeta, often referred to as "water silk" because of the wavy effect embossed on the surface.	Fair to Bad	Fair	Good
Noil Silk	Soft, slightly nubby fabric that has a cottonlike appearance. Sportswear fabric at a moderate price.	Good to Fair	Fair	Good
Taffeta	Plain weave silk with a crisp hand and a soft luster. Found in many different weights, solid or printed.	Bad	Bad	Good
Twill	A type of weave found in silk, wool, cotton, and blends. It has a fine pronounced diagonal rib. Found in suit weights.	Fair to Bad	Fair	Good
Velvet	A large family of soft, rich, thick woven pile fabrics with a plushy surface. Also comes in cotton and synthetic blends.	Fair	Fair	Pile can be crushed permanently with friction. It is also the first thing to wear away.
Wool and Wool Blend	Light- to heavyweight fabric with a springy hand and a low lustrous sheen that 100% wool does not have. Great insulation qualities.	Fair	Good	Good

SILK BLENDS

BREATHABILITY	WASHING INSTRUCTIONS	IRONING INSTRUCTIONS
Good	Dry-clean only. Chiffon should never be immersed in water because it will shrink.	Test heat and pressure on a scrap or tiny area of fabric. Use steam with discretion as very sheer fabrics may shrink and pucker.
Good	Light-colored solids are hand-washable. Dark, bright, or printed fabrics should be dry-cleaned.	Dry-iron on wrong side of garment.
Good	Dry-clean only.	Dry-iron on the wrong side is advised. Use press cloth. Do not overpress as the pebbly texture will be flattened.
Excellent	Light-colored solids are hand-washable with great care due to the fragility of the open weave. Dark, bright, or printed fabrics should be dry-cleaned.	Dry-iron on wrong side of dampened garment.
Good	Dry-clean only.	This fabric is generally heat-sensitive due to metal threads which could dull, melt, or tarnish from excessive heat.
Good	Dry-clean only.	Use warm, dry iron and a gentle light touch. Steam may cause permanent puckers or dulled fibers.
Good	Hand-washable. Test small swatch of fabric to make sure color does not run or fade.	Dry-iron on the wrong side of a dampened garment.
Fair	Dry-clean only. Tends to shrink and stiffen when wet.	Use warm, dry iron and a gentle light touch. Steam may cause permanent puckers or dulled fibers.
Good	Because of the pronounced diagonal texture, soil is not as visible on the surface of this fabric. Dry-clean only.	Use warm, dry iron on a damp garment, on the wrong side. Press lightly so as not to flatten texture.
Good	Dry-clean only. Never crowd velvet in a closet—pile is easily crushed. Store by pinning garment on hanger—folding crushes nap.	To remove wrinkles, put garment on a padded hanger and take into the bathroom. Let it hang while you shower. Steam should remove wrinkles.
Good	Light-colored solids are hand-washable. Dark, bright, or printed fabrics should be dry-cleaned.	Use warm, dry iron on a damp garment on the wrong side.

in this chapter. Iron while the garment is still damp. Press it on the wrong side, to avoid shine. For best results, when ironing a dry garment, dampen it and put it in a pillowcase or fabric bag in your refrigerator for an hour. When you take it out, you'll find ironing a breeze. Don't use a steam iron unless it's new or very clean. Rust often collects in the steam holes and can leave marks or stains on the garment.

To remove grease stains from white or pastel silks, use white blotting paper, available at most stationery stores, and white tailor's chalk, available in fabric stores and five-and-dime stores. Using a single-edged razor blade or paring knife, shave the chalk and let the powder fall on the stain. Place pieces of blotting paper under and over the spot, and touch the top paper with a warm iron. The heat of the iron will blot out the grease without leaving a stain.

COTTON

Cotton continues to be one of the most important natural fibers because its trans-seasonal usefulness and innovative blends make it so versatile. Because of the wide range of finishing processes that alter its appearance, cotton

COTTON AND

FABRIC	DESCRIPTION	DRAPABILITY	CREASE RESISTANCE	FRICTION RESISTANCE
Broadcloth	A fine, smooth, sporty cloth in a plain weave. So called because it came in widths over a yard.	Fair	Fair	Good
Chintz	A solid or printed cloth with a shiny glazed finish which from afar looks similar to leather.	Has body of its own. Fair to Bad	Fair	The glazed finish wears off in abrasive areas and frequently the fabric will lose its shine as the finish is not always durable.
Crêpe	French word meaning "crinkle." A rough, pebbly surface of highly twisted yarns characterizes this fabric.	Good	Good	Good
Duck	A cotton cloth somewhat like canvas, but finer and lighter in weight. Also found in linen.	Bad	Fair to Bad	Good

is in great demand. One type of finishing—sizing—is put into cotton shirting fabrics. Sizing is a complex starch, similar to the simpler starches women use at home, and is not necessarily permanent. When it washes out (in cheap garments, after one or two launderings), it leaves a flimsy garment without the body it had originally.

Cotton can be stiffened, glazed, raised, mercerized (a luster-giving process), and waterproofed. Recent developments are coated cotton rainwear, cotton pile sweatsuits, and cotton polished to the luster and smoothness of silk. Blends of cotton with hairy, shiny, or textured fibers create various visual effects not usually associated with cotton.

Cotton is extremely durable and strong. Unlike silk and wool, cotton is much stronger wet than dry, and can be handled roughly during laundering. Because of its easy washability and low cost, compared to other natural fibers, cotton is in great demand for playclothes, uniforms, and other garments that are expected to take a lot of wear and rough treatment. Cotton has good absorbency and conducts heat well.

Cotton stains easily and is harmed by mineral acids, so spots and stains must be removed immediately. More detailed instructions for care of cottons and cotton blends follow.

COTTON BLENDS

BREATHABILITY	WASHING INSTRUCTIONS	IRONING INSTRUCTIONS
Good	Light-colored solids are hand-washable. Caution should be taken as colors can fade or bleed if not colorfast. First test a small area or swatch.	Most cottons have a high heat resistance. We advise dampening the garment and using a dry iron, as often rust deposits in the holes of steam irons and can stain the garment.
Fair	Hand-washing will wear off the glazed finish more rapidly than dry-cleaning solvents.	Iron on wrong side at about 300° F, lower than the setting for 100% cotton, so as not to scorch, pucker, or melt finish or fabric.
Good	Dry-cleaning preferable.	Dry-iron on the wrong side of a dampened garment. Use press cloth. Do not overpress, as it will flatten the pebbly texture.
Good	Can be hand-washed or machine-washed but test fabric first to assure that color will not bleed or run.	Use warm, dry iron on a damp garment, on wrong side. A steam iron may be used, but make sure it is clean.

FABRIC	DESCRIPTION	DRAPABILITY	CREASE RESISTANCE	FRICTION RESISTANCE
Flannelette	A lofty, lightweight, loosely woven fabric that has a soft and fuzzy texture.	Good	Good	Good
Muslin	A fine cotton cloth with a plain weave and a terrific affinity for dyes.	Excellent	Fair	Good
Oxford	Heavier than broadcloth, it is made with a fine warp and a heavy filling yarn which gives a full, tightly woven heavy side to the fabric.	Fair	Fair	Good
Piqué	A combed yarn fabric with narrow raised cords running lengthwise. Pinwale—very narrow cord material. Waffle piqué—honeycomb-textured fabric.	Fair	Fair	Fair
Polyester and Cotton Blend	Blended with cotton, polyester improves the washability and ease of care of the fabric, but it does cut down on the warmth.	Fair	Good to Excellent	Good to Excellent
Silk and Cotton Blend	A springy, wrinkle-resistant blend which resembles 100% cotton with a low, rich luster.	Good	Fair	Good
Terry Cloth (often blended with polyester)	A pile fabric with uncut loops and a dense, plushy ground cover.	Fair	Good	Pile will snag, pull, and wear away with friction. Fair to Good
Twill (2 types) Gabardine Herringbone	Twills have a prominent diagonal rib and a right and wrong side. Gabardine—a lengthwise-faced steep twill with very prominent wales. Herringbone—a fabric with a twill line reversed at regular intervals.	Fair to Bad	Good	Good
Voile	Also referred to as "cheesecloth" and "gauze." A loosely woven, soft, light, plain weave fabric with a low thread count that gives these fabrics a transparent look.	Good to Excellent	Fair to Bad	Good

COTTON BLENDS

BREATHABILITY	WASHING INSTRUCTIONS	IRONING INSTRUCTIONS
Good	Can be hand-washed or machine-washed but test fabric first to assure that color will not bleed or run.	Use warm, dry iron on a damp garment, on wrong side. A steam iron may be used, but make sure it is clean.
Good	Machine-washable, but note that this fabric is known to shrink drastically if not treated with a special finish. Also test to assure that colors do not bleed.	″
Good	Light-colored solids can be hand-washed. We advise dry cleaning bright or dark colors which may bleed or fade.	″
Fair	″	″ Overpressing will flatten the ribbed texture.
Fair	Hand- and machine-washable. When laundering, use "fragile" setting.	Iron at a lower setting than cotton. Polyester is heat-sensitive. This blend requires less ironing because of polyester's ease of care.
Good	Light-colored solids can be hand-washed. We advise dry-cleaning bright or dark colors which may bleed or fade.	Use warm, dry iron on a damp garment, on wrong side. A steam iron may be used, but make sure it is clean.
Good	Hand- and machine-washable. When laundering, use "fragile" setting. Test swatch first to assure that fabric will not bleed or run.	Press with minimum pressure on the wrong side, using a press cloth. Flattening the pile will cause the fabric to appear lighter in color.
Good	Dry-clean.	″ Press lightly so as not to flatten the rib or feathered texture of the herringbone fabric.
Good	Hand-wash with care because of loose, open weave. Test swatch first to assure that fabric will not bleed or run.	Use warm, dry iron on a damp garment on wrong side. A steam iron may be used, but make sure it is clean.

LINEN

Linen, a vegetable fiber made from the flax plant, has been a prestige fabric since the time of the pharaohs. Because of its limited production, linen is relatively expensive. This exquisite fabric has little resiliency and tends to wrinkle at a glance. (Perhaps this was the reason why Saks had to reduce its men's designer linen shirts during a summer sale from $50 to $9.90.) Fabric manufacturers have developed many crease-resistant finishes for linen, but they reduce the fabric's durability and breathability.

Linen is very strong—twice as strong as cotton, and much stronger than cotton when it is wet. It can be washed roughly by hand without damaging it. Stains are easier to remove from linen than from cotton, and it is more resistant to mildew than cotton is. Like cotton, linen will fade, yellow, and discolor when it is exposed to prolonged sunlight.

Like silk and cotton, linen should be ironed with a dry iron while it is quite damp. Ironing on the right side of the fabric will increase linen's luster.

Linen varies from very lightweight handkerchief fabrics to tailorable suiting weights. Its texture can be smooth and flat or coarse and nubby, depending on the thickness of the fiber, how it is twisted during spinning, the weave, and the finishing.

Linen can be blended with synthetic fabrics to create easy-care fabrics

LINEN AND

FABRIC	DESCRIPTION	DRAPABILITY	CREASE RESISTANCE	FRICTION RESISTANCE
Linen	A vegetable fiber from the flax plant spun and woven into a variety of different-weight fabrics.	Depends upon weight. Fair	Bad	Good
Handkerchief Linen	A very fine lightweight gauze-like fabric with a very low thread count. Somewhat transparent.	Fair to Good	Bad	Good
Cotton and Linen Blend	Depending upon the proportions of cotton and linen, this blend can vary from light- to heavy-weight. It is moderate in price and as durable as its components.	Fair	Fair to Bad	Good. Linen is twice as strong as cotton, creating a durable blend.
Polyester and Linen Blend	A blend that is less expensive than the prestigious natural fiber and also more wrinkle resistant.	Fair	Good	Good
Silk and Linen Blend	Silk adds a lustrous sheen and smoothness to this strong, durable fiber.	Good	Fair to Bad	Good

with the best properties of both natural and man-made fibers. Linen with polyester wrinkles far less than pure linen. Linen can be blended with silk for a dressier, lustrous fabric, or with cotton for a sportier effect.

MAN-MADE FIBERS

Man-made fibers are certainly a wonder of the twentieth century. They are everything-proof: crease-, wrinkle-, water-, and age-resistant. These synthetic chemical creations are very versatile, but they lack the beauty and durability of natural fibers—they're only imitations.

Synthetics are very heat-sensitive. A high setting on your iron can shrink and melt the fabric. Because of their low moisture absorbency, they are much less comfortable than natural fibers in warm and humid weather. Synthetics are difficult to dye because they resist water.

Synthetics are very strong and can take a beating without showing it. They are very static and often cling and collect lint, which makes them look messy and dirty very rapidly. These man-made fibers—the acrylics, nylons, and polyesters—can be wonderful for travel because they require little or no ironing. Yet, although synthetics are convenient for women on the go, we do not feel that they can compare with the luxury and beauty of natural and natural-blend fabrics, and cannot recommend them wholeheartedly.

LINEN BLENDS

BREATHABILITY	WASHING INSTRUCTIONS	IRONING INSTRUCTIONS
Good	Hand-wash light-colored solids. Dark, bright, or printed fabrics should be dry-cleaned. Do not twist or wring when hand-washing.	Dry-iron a very damp garment on the wrong side. Ironing on right side will increase the luster.
Good	"	"
Good	"	"
Fair	Polyester and linen are both extremely strong fibers. These fabrics are washable. We advise testing a small area first for running or bleeding.	Iron this blend at a lower temperature due to polyester's sensitivity to heat.
Good	Dry-clean only.	Dry-iron a dampened garment on the wrong side.

FABRIC	DESCRIPTION	DRAPABILITY	CREASE RESISTANCE	FRICTION RESISTANCE
Acetate (*2 kinds*) *Diacetates Triacetates*	A man-made cellulose fiber often used in tricots. It has many silklike qualities and is used in many silklike garments.	Good to Excellent	Good	Sensitive to abrasion when wet.
Acrylic	A synthetic fiber with a soft, woolly hand. Very resilient, with an excellent resistance to sunlight.	Fair	Excellent	Fair to Good
Metallics	Novelty fabrics with beads, sequins, gold or silver thread woven in. These fabrics often have an iridescent quality and reflect light.	Depends upon weight. Fair to Good	Fair	Must be careful. Friction will tend to wear away metal threads. Beads and sequins will fall off.
Nylon	A practical and inexpensive fiber usually turned into a slinky, clingy fabric. Nylon is a familiar component of knit fabrics, often very static.	Good	Good to Excellent	Good
Polyester	Frequently found in knits, this fiber contributes qualities of strength and ease of care. The most widely used synthetic fiber. Good resistance to sunlight.	Fair to Bad	Excellent	Polyester, like wool, will "pill," but the balls that accumulate on the fabric are very difficult to remove. Also a very static fabric.
Rayon-Viscose	Fabric manufacturers can weave and finish rayon so it resembles—in hand and beauty—either silk, linen, or wool. Very versatile, low-cost, and seasonless fabric.	Good to Excellent	Good	Good. Nonstatic fabric
Spandex	A synthetic fiber developed for its stretch properties. Used in lingerie and active sportswear. Excellent recovery characteristics.	Fair—best for body-molding styles	Good to Excellent	Good to Excellent

FIBERS

TRADE-MARKS	BREATH-ABILITY	WASHING INSTRUCTIONS	IRONING INSTRUCTIONS
Arnel Celanese Avisco Estron	Fair	We advise dry-cleaning as colors may fade. This synthetic fiber does not have the ease of care of most man-made fibers. Both fibers have very little resiliency.	Acetates are highly flammable. They are not very durable and will melt if the iron is too hot.
Orlon Acrilan Zefran Creslan	Fair	Washes well in machine or dry-clean.	Iron at 300° F. Watch iron's heat as this fiber will shrivel and melt if too hot.
Lurex Fairtex Mylar	Depends upon fiber content. Fair to Good	Dry-clean anything sequined, beaded, or woven with metal threads. They could discolor, rust, or tarnish if washed by hand.	These fabrics generally require professional care. Ironing may melt or tarnish sequins, beads, or metal threads. Avoid steam because of discoloration. Do not fold metallics as they may crack or peel.
Antron Enkalure Qiana Celanese	Fair	Avoid stretching or twisting nylon when hand-washing. Harsh or careless washing methods can discolor nylon. Do not leave soaking as the fabric will lose strength, body, and shape.	Excess heat causes discoloration. Iron at a low heat setting and test a small area first.
Dacron Avlin Fortrel Trevira Kodel	Not comfortable in hot, humid weather. Fiber does not breathe.	Because of the fiber's static quality it tends to attract lint and soils rapidly. The fabric is very washable, because of low moisture absorbency. This fabric dries very quickly and machine-washes beautifully.	Safe ironing temperature 325° F. Polyester will melt if the iron is too hot.
Enka Fortisan Furilon	Good	Should be dry-cleaned to retain size and appearance. Less apt to fade, can crock and bleed in washing. Easy dyeability as it absorbs moisture well and is very comfortable in humid weather.	Rayon, like cotton, is flammable. Iron at a cotton setting or lower, depending upon fabric weight. Excess heat can cause scorching.
Lycra Vyrene	Fair	Good resistance to laundering and dry-cleaning solvents. Chlorine bleaches will cause yellowing.	Because of the wonderful recovery factor of this fabric, it requires virtually no ironing.

KNITS

Knits are made of fiber discussed elsewhere in this chapter, but knits' unique properties deserve a section all their own. With the wondrously innovative combinations of natural and man-made fibers, designers and even adventurous hand-knitters are creating beautiful and unconventional new design ideas. Knits have three basic properties: elasticity, stretch, resiliency. The loop structure of knits makes them drape well, but they're bulkier than woven fabric and not as stable. Knits are less rigid than woven fabrics. Knits are also more porous than woven fabric: air can pass more freely through knits than through woven cloth. Knits are less subject to wrinkling and mussing than woven fabrics.

Because of knits' unique structural advantages and insulating qualities, knits will be hot fashion in the fuel-conscious 1980s. Recently the market has been flooded with Fair Isles, argyles, Aran Isles, cable patterns, and fancy handknits.

Knit Construction

Knitted garments can be constructed in several ways and the different techniques determine the fit, quality, and price of the garment. We often see "full fashion" on the hangtag of a sweater. This term refers to a garment that is completely knitted to its finished shape on a knitting or industrial machine. This is the way a hand-knitter knits a sweater; this method signifies quality and care in construction and a better fit. "Cut-and-sew" garments, on the other hand, are knitted on machines just like knitted cloth yardage; the pieces are then cut and sewed together ("merrowed") like fabric. The process is much quicker and therefore cheaper, even though it produces more waste.

"Handknit" means that the garment has been made on a hand-knitting machine—not necessarily that it was made by hand. These are generally the most ornate and expensive knitted garments.

PAGE 79: *New shapes—yarns—colors and stitches add excitement in knitwear.*
CENTRAL FIGURE: *A bold abstract sweater in a geometric motif.*
TOP LEFT: *A classic Aran Isle knit in a tunic sweater.*
TOP CENTER: *Intricate "retro"-style jacquard.*
TOP RIGHT: *Sporty elegance in this unexpectedly large argyle.*
CENTER LEFT: *Fair Isle-inspired long blouson cardigan.*
CENTER RIGHT: *Elephant jacquard in a bold jungle look.*
BOTTOM: *Norwegian-style jacquard sweater with Scandinavian geometric motifs.*

SUEDE AND LEATHER

Suede and leather are both durable luxury fibers. They have gained enormous recognition with the most avant-garde fashion trends, like the punk and cosmic styles of the late 1970s and the 1980s, and are the favorites of more conservative designers because they make strong, elegant fashion statements.

Many women love leather and suede, but don't know how to care for them and inadvertently abuse them. Leather was not meant to be a raincoat, and suede needs regular brushing. They should not be neglected; sooner or later, lack of care will show.

Leather is a strong, flexible fiber with a spongy structure. It is very warm and extremely comfortable. The fiber's relative elasticity enables designers to put it to many uses. Norma Kamali has even used it for beachwear (for sunning, not swimming), and Claude Montana, king of innovative leather creations, has designed leather-appliquéd dresses, leather-backed snap tops, and even leather shorts. Leather can be punched or sprinkled with nailheads, as Calvin Klein did, or used in "collage-dressing" designs, as England's Zandra Rhodes and Thea Porter have done.

Retain leather's beauty by cleaning and conditioning it regularly. Light surface dirt can be removed easily with a clean damp cloth and mild soap. *Never use cleaning fluids or harsh detergents—they can ruin leather's fine finish.* Leather is porous and must breathe. *Never wrap it in plastic* or you may have an unsightly, discolored garment. Keep leather clothes in a cool, well-ventilated area, since heat can bake leather and make it turn hard, stiff, and brittle. Protect leather from dust in cloth garment bags.

If you're caught in a downpour and your leather coat gets soaked, hang it on a padded hanger. For extra TLC, stuff the sleeves with tissue paper and let the coat dry overnight at room temperature to preserve its suppleness. *Never leave leather near the radiator—you'll destroy it.*

Suede requires even more care and attention than leather because it can get water-spotted. Mild surface dirt can be removed with a soap eraser. Brush suede often with a suede brush, rubber sponge, or terrycloth towel to keep dirt from setting. Like leather, suede needs to breathe. Air it out regularly, but out of direct sunlight, and store it in cloth garment bags. If your suede garment gets caught in the rain, dry it as though it were leather. After it is dry, perk up the nap with a soft brush or rubber sponge.

Clean leather and suede professionally when they get heavily soiled.

Leather specialists can recondition your garments completely at reasonable rates.

FUR

Fur is the designers' darling. In the past ten years, advanced technology has opened up an enormous range of design possibilities. Fur can be dyed any color, cut, appliquéd, ribbed like corduroy, woven, as Perry Ellis did, or draped, as the inventive Fendi sisters do it.

Whether your fur is a new acquisition or used to be your grandmother's best coat, treat it carefully so that it remains in good condition. Always hang furs on a sturdy long-necked, padded hanger, away from direct sunlight. Like other natural fibers, fur needs to breathe. Don't crowd it in a closet. And never use plastic, which can dry the skins, "sunburn" the fur, and age it prematurely.

If you're caught in a storm or a blizzard, don't panic. Fur takes to wetness better than you think. (Remember: it used to protect the animal underneath.) It's only when the leather underneath or the lining gets soaked that it's time to see a professional furrier. Don't turn the coat inside-out to protect it; linings are usually more fragile than the fur. Slightly wet furs should be treated like wet leather or suede.

Furs should be stored professionally from spring to fall, but not cleaned every year. Bill Waxler, our favorite furrier, who sells millions of dollars worth of furs every year, says that not only isn't it necessary to clean your furs every year, but that it also ages them prematurely. Depending on how often you wear them, the severity of the winters and the air pollution where you live, cleaning may be necessary only every three or five years. He thinks that the best thing to do for your furs is to wear them because body heat helps maintain the shape of the garment. He urges women to wear their furs as often as they like, rather than letting them age in the closet.

Furs are relatively strong and require little more attention and care than other natural fibers. Take care of your furs, hang and store them properly, and they will remain lustrous and beautiful for many years.

5
How to Judge Tailoring

A FTER FABRIC, tailoring is the most important element of a garment. Even with the most exquisite fabric, a garment's fit depends on how it is made, and looks terrific only when the style, construction, and finishing do not draw attention to a single detail of the garment and exaggerate it, but rather enhance its overall look. How a garment is made has a major impact on the way you look. Bosses—and that usually means men—are hypersensitive to both good and hideous tailoring. They may be relatively oblivious to the subtleties of fabric, but they're very aware of good tailoring because it's an executive "caste mark."

After you've found a style that suits you, the next checkpoint is its tailoring and finishing. Fashions can be "knocked off," styles and fabrics copied, but good workmanship is either there or not there, and it usually costs money. Extra time and added care are necessary to create quality in a finished garment. Here are some tailoring points that you should check before you pull out your wallet:

FABRIC GRAIN must be balanced in order for the lines of a garment to
       fall beautifully. (We'll go into a complete discussion of grain
       a little later in this chapter.)

82

LININGS should not bubble, pull, or pucker; these tailoring flaws make the garment uncomfortable to wear.

SHOULDER SEAMS should be positioned correctly and identically.

NECKLINES should hug the body and fall flatly over the shoulder-neck area.

PLEATS, GATHERS, VENTS, and TUCKS should be even (none larger or smaller than the others) and should hang correctly and smoothly.

POCKETS, PIPING, TOPSTITCHING, and any decorative trim should work with the style of the garment and should be positioned properly on the garment and on your body.

COLLARS, CUFFS, BODICE, and WAISTBAND should be pressed so that they sit flat on the garment without gapping, pulling, puckering, or rippling.

PANTS should have adequate space in the crotch.

EVERY GARMENT should be cut to allow ease of movement and should be finished according to the fabric's weight and garment's style in order to enhance its overall look.

General construction details deserve particular attention. Of these, one of the most important is the grain of the fabric.

GRAIN

The grain of the fabric is one of its most important components. The grain of the fabric refers to the position of both the lengthwise and crosswise yarns. It is essential that a garment be cut carefully "on-grain," hanging perpendicular to the floor. Otherwise the garment will hang slightly askew and will tend to twist and sag. Seams may eventually pull and pucker. These construction details cannot be overlooked.

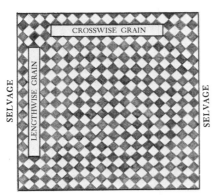

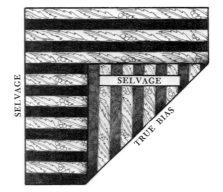

CROSSWISE FOLD

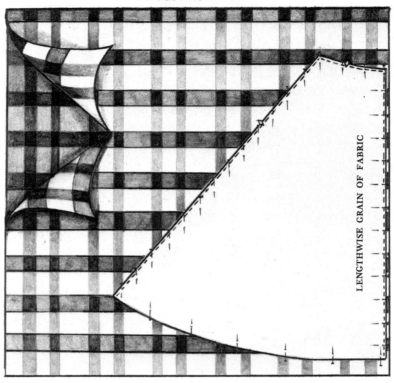

LENGTHWISE GRAIN OF FABRIC

Use the center seams and pre-dominant stripes of the plaid as your guide when matching uneven lengthwise plaids.

In plaids and stripes, cutting "off the grain" is much more obvious because horizontal and vertical lines won't match. The alignment of grains is essential to the drape of a well-made garment.

Plaids, stripes, large floral patterns, and border prints must be placed and pieced strategically when manufacturers make a garment. The first thing we notice in a cheap or carelessly made garment is an unmatched plaid or stripe, a large print with an unnecessary seam through it, or an unevenly matched border print. Watch for these construction details when choosing a garment. They require added care and distinguish a quality garment from a quick and careless knock-off job.

Good plaid garments should match exactly in color and stripe at all seam meetings. The fewer the seams, the easier it is to match plaids. Because the pattern has to be positioned just right, more fabric is required, and this makes the garment more expensive. But it's worth it! Hemlines in plaids should be placed on the bottom of a completed block of plaid; this line tends

MATCHING PLAIDS AND STRIPES IS ESSENTIAL TO
A SUCCESSFUL GARMENT.

INCORRECT   **CORRECT**

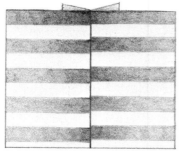 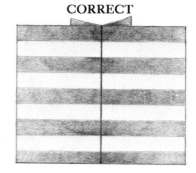

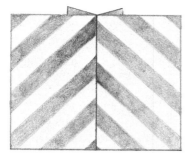 

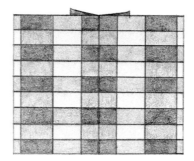

to have a more tailored and finished look, rather than cutting a block of plaid without attention to its regularity or irregularity.

Stripes are not as difficult for manufacturers to handle because the design runs in only one direction. But, like plaids, they can look absolutely disastrous if they do not meet correctly.

Floral patterns have to be positioned carefully, too. Since they often have a one-way pattern—for example, a flower on a stem—all pattern pieces must be placed in the same direction. Garments with large floral prints should have a minimum number of seams. Too many seams will break up the motifs and detract from the fabric's beauty. It is often very difficult to lay out small pattern pieces of a complicatedly cut garment on a large printed fabric, and it generally doesn't make a successful, attractive piece of clothing.

Pile fabrics, such as corduroy, velvet, and velveteen, have a dense ground cover and require special care when they are sewed, much like large plaids and florals. Because pile is directional and looks different whether it is held up or down, all the pattern pieces have to be placed going in the same direction. To determine the direction of the pile, move your hand lightly over the fabric. If the surface is smooth, you are going with the pile; and if your hand is moving roughly, brushing the fibers upward, you are going against the pile. Make sure that the direction of the pile is the same all through the garment; otherwise, different pattern pieces will appear to be different colors under varying lighting conditions.

Napped fabrics have fibers that are raised from the body of the cloth. These fibers are then brushed, for a soft effect, or flattened to give a sheen to fabrics like cashmere, flannel, fleece, and wool broadcloth. In these fabrics, the fibers' direction is more visible. Manufacturers should cut these fabrics with the nap running downward. Again, all pattern pieces should be placed in the same direction.

FINISHING AND SEAMS

The best way to determine the quality of a garment is to first get a taste of the best. Go to a luxury department store in your area and browse through the designer department. Don't be scared or intimidated by the atmosphere. (On the other hand, don't dress grubbily, either.) Look inside the garments. Pay attention to seam finishings, closures, linings, hems, and stitching. You'll quickly realize the difference between quality finishing and none at all. And while you may not be able to afford designer clothes now, you'll become aware of what makes good tailoring and you'll recognize it when you see it in sale garments and snap it up.

Careful construction is essential to the appearance of a plaid or stripe garment.

NOTE: *Vertical stripes elongate; plaids add width.*

Properly formed seams should be nearly invisible. The seam finishing and type of seam is determined by the fabric used and the style of the garment. Sheer fabrics often require *double-stitched seams*, which add strength and prevent fraying. *French seams* are used for washable sheers. This finishing is excellent for most lightweight fabrics because it gives a very clean, well-tailored look to the inside of the garment.

Seams can be finished in several different ways. *Pinked seams* can be used on fabric that will not fray or ravel. (Wool and cotton jerseys are good examples.) Seams can be bound with seam binding, which is tacked down to each side of the seam to cover the raw edges. This finishing is excellent for unconstructed jackets and coats. *Bound seams* are usually used for fabrics that fray: tweeds, heavy linens, and coarse weaves. Seams can be *overcast* to prevent fraying; sometimes they are *machine-finished*. Often commercial garments have *merrowed edges* to prevent their raveling.

For decoration, a seam can be *topstitched*. When topstitching is gone over many times, the fabric takes on a stiffer, finished effect.

There are many techniques for finishing seams. The decision is determined by the designer's choice of fabric and the detail in the cut and construction of the garment.

Sometimes a good seam is ruined by a bad pressing. This is easy to notice and easy to fix. Follow the ironing directions in the fabric charts in Chapter 4, and always use a press cloth.

LININGS

Linings drastically affect the look and fit of a garment. The way the lining fits is an essential part of achieving a durable, attractive garment. Linings must be tailored just as thoroughly as the outer garment, and we feel that an equal amount of care should be given to the inside construction. Ideally, a lining should be slightly smaller than the garment itself, and it should be of comparable weight, so that the fabric will not distort the look of the garment. For example, a sheer organza makes an ideal underlining for silks and wool crêpes. China silk and SiBonne are also suitable for closely woven wools and raw silks.

When you examine a garment, look first at the outside for any rippling, pulling, or sagging. Often linings are put in too tightly and may cause rippling of the outside fabric. This can happen even in better clothing. Today many designers are attaching the linings all along the outer fabric. Therefore, if the lining is not placed and sewn perfectly, sooner or later it may start to pull

FINISHING AND SEAMS

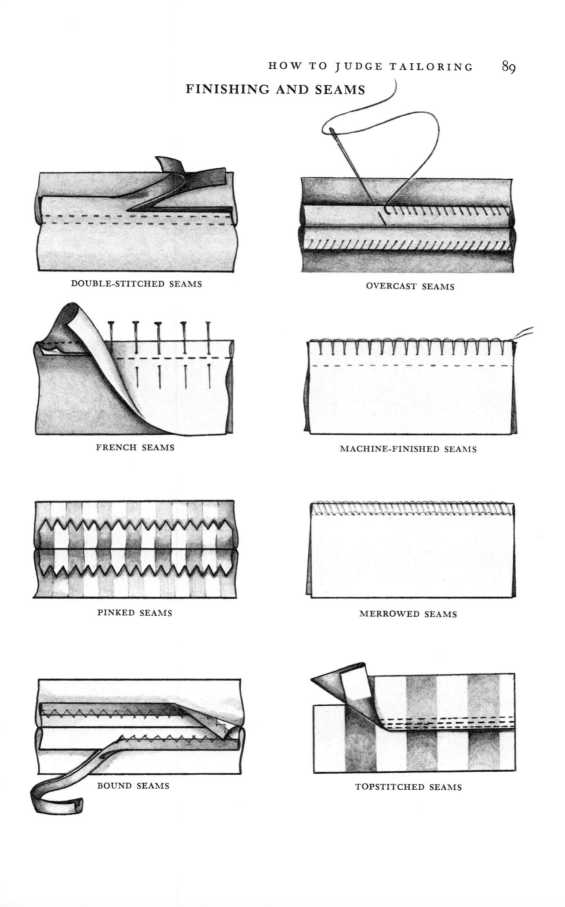

DOUBLE-STITCHED SEAMS

OVERCAST SEAMS

FRENCH SEAMS

MACHINE-FINISHED SEAMS

PINKED SEAMS

MERROWED SEAMS

BOUND SEAMS

TOPSTITCHED SEAMS

the outer fabric. This sort of rippling is often visible on coats and jackets and is much more difficult to correct than linings which are tacked at key points rather than completely sewed. As we always caution, take a good look in a three-way mirror and carefully inspect the inside and outside of your garment before you buy it and walk out of the store with it.

HEMS

All eyes tend to focus on a carelessly made hem, so make sure to inspect the hem of a garment for any unevenness, sloping, puckering, rippling, or poor stitching before you buy it. (Most hems are easy to redo. Therefore, if you love a skirt or dress but the hem is poorly made, it may still be worth buying. However, since we feel that good and poor tailoring are consistent within a garment, make sure that the hem is the only flaw in an otherwise wonderful piece of clothing.)

Since there are no set lengths and designers seem to feel that anywhere from several inches above the knee to several inches above the ankle is fair game, the only advice we can give you is not to be overly influenced by any designer's fashion trends. Decide on a length, or range of lengths, that suits your height. Remember to keep your shoe/boot/sandal height and fashion accessories in mind; they will all affect the look you want to project. The best hem length is the one that compliments your figure and creates a look that makes you feel comfortable and confident.

Style and fabric dictate the way in which a hem is finished. No matter which technique is used, the hem should always fall smoothly. Stitches should be invisible unless they are part of the hem's decorative effect. The depth of the hem itself can vary from less than 1″ to up to 10″, depending on the

THE HEM
Final key to a successful garment

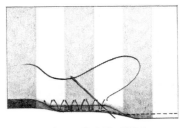

HAND-ROLLED HEM

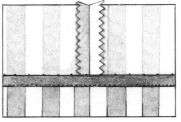

BIAS-BOUND HEM

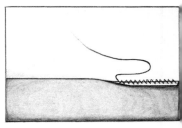

BLINDSTITCHED HEM

desired look and weight of the fabric. A slim skirt usually requires a deeper hem than a full skirt. Certain fabrics require special finishing techniques. Delicate fabrics like chiffon, lace, sheer wool, and other very lightweight fabrics can be finished with *hand-rolled hems*. Although this type of hem finishing is found most often on scarves, it is a sign of care and quality workmanship when it is used on the hem, neckline, or cuff of a garment.

Bias binding of either silk or rayon is often used on the hems of heavy or napped woolen fabrics. This binding provides a stability and tailored finish to heavy hems. *Blindstitched hem finishing*, we feel, is the most frequently used technique and provides a durable, attractive finish. It is suitable for most lightweight fabrics and for full and straight skirts.

These are a few techniques used in the last steps of finishing a garment. We feel that every part of a garment must work together harmoniously. No one area should attract attention because of careless workmanship or improper placement. Here again, have a good three-way mirror and/or an eagle-eyed friend handy whenever you're shopping for clothes.

Here are a few more construction details to focus on:

ZIPPERS

Zippers must be put in well. They should generally be concealed; in fact, we usually recommend taking them out and putting them in by hand. Industrial zippers are the exception. They are supposed to be visible and are usually a decorative element of the garment's design.

POCKETS

Check pocket placement and depth. Jam your hands in the pockets and move around. How does the garment look? How does it feel? How do you feel? Look for any lumps, bulges, or distortion of the fabric. Haven't we all had the experience of buying a beautiful pair of pants or an exquisite slim skirt with pockets that only an infant's hand would fit into. Either the designer and manufacturer had skimped on the fabric or hadn't fit the garment on a model to see that the pocket height and depth worked. Bad pocket design and placement are mistakes that often happen and destroy the pockets' function. Bad pockets should be removed; we'll show you how in the next chapter.

Pocket fabric should be lightweight so that it doesn't show through the garment. Designers often have to search the fabric market for the correct color and weight of fabric for the pocket interior for their designs. This is another important (and often overlooked) aspect in the creation of a garment and can ruin a look if it is done carelessly. Nothing is uglier than the outline of a large pocket showing gaily through a pair of flannel pants. Fit and fabric weight determine what type of fabric should be used for pockets. Sometimes the same fabric as the garment can be used, but not always. The acid test is how clothes look in a mirror.

BUTTONS AND BUTTONHOLES

Buttons and buttonholes, like many other parts of a garment, can add beauty, quality, and a certain look to a garment if they are selected and finished correctly. Buttons and buttonholes can be decorative as well as functional. They must be positioned properly to contribute to the fit and comfort of a garment, as well as its appearance. Because of faulty placement of buttons and buttonholes, blouse fronts can gap and pull. Minute differences in placement can drastically alter the look of a garment.

Placing the buttonholes requires time and care; it is essential for a successful garment. Buttonholes should not be too small to put the button through without ruining a manicure, or so large that they pop open if you merely turn a doorknob. The three key points for positioning buttonholes are the fullest part of the bust, the neckline, and the waistline; remaining buttons are spaced between these points.

Check that buttons are sewn on properly, or plan to resew them yourself if they are not. Lightweight fabrics need small buttons sewed on fairly closely with fine thread. Heavy tweeds and coating fabrics need large buttons sewed on with heavy thread; there's a special weight just for this purpose. There should be enough thread between the button and the fabric so that the button has some play. Thread should be wrapped around the shank of the button to reinforce it.

Care in finishing a garment distinguishes a quality, well-made, and well-fitting garment from a careless, botched-looking piece of clothing. Educate your eye to distinguish them—it pays!

KNITS

Judging the construction of knits is similar to judging the construction of woven cloth, but there are additional construction details to focus attention on. Knits have a wonderful stretch recovery, which makes them excellent for fitted and body-molding styles. Make sure that the garment you're selecting has elasticity and that it bounces back to its original shape. Look for a cleanly finished garment; there shouldn't be any yarn hanging from the inner seams. Make sure that there are no dropped stitches or visible flaws in the knitting.

Check the sleeve lengths; they should be identical. (They aren't always.)

If you're trying on a cardigan, make sure the buttons and buttonholes are aligned correctly and that there is no puckering or pulling down the center front. Check all the knitting measurements to make sure they are even and balanced (fold the garment in half) unless the design is clearly and deliberately asymmetric.

Because the preppie look has swept the country from college campuses to designer showrooms, lots of badly made shetlands are flooding the country. Here's how to avoid them: Shetlands should have a lofty, soft feel; only a bad shetland will feel itchy. (You may plan to wear shetlands only over cotton and silk shirts, but we recommend trying them on over just a bra in order to check their quality.) Shop the men's and boys' department for these classic looks; they're often cheaper than women's sweaters, and they're almost always made better.

Cashmere, another classic of investment dressing, is a major investment and requires some knowledge, now that a good sweater can cost a week's salary. Good cashmere should not be fuzzy. A quality garment should be at least two-ply; three- and four-ply are for outdoor wear, and are astronomical. (We saw a four-ply crew neck in a simple cream rib for $350 at a good New York men's store.) We stress men's sweaters—especially cashmeres—because they're usually knitted on smaller needles. This creates a heavier, more stable sweater, with more stitches, and more cashmere, to the square inch. If you can find a man's sweater that fits you, you'll be getting more cashmere—and long wear—for your money.

There's a lot to be aware of and to look for when you're shopping for clothes. At times it can seem overwhelming. But if you keep your eyes open, you'll learn quickly and you'll build on your experience. If you're ever uncertain or undecided, don't buy the garment. We've all regretted a few things that we saw and didn't buy, but how many more things have we regretted buying!

6
What's Alterable, What Isn't

THE CLOTHES WE wear reflect our spirit, our temperament, and our view of life. We can tell a lot about a woman by the way she puts her clothes together, the condition of her clothing, and whether it suits her figure —all of which express her personality, attitude, and self-image.

Often small alterations in clothing can make drastic differences in your personal look and will affect the way people react to you. The simplest alterations, like raising or lowering a hem, taking in or letting out side seams, or removing trimming or pockets can change the look of a garment, thus creating a style or silhouette more suited to your personal taste and figure.

Sometimes you're tempted to buy a garment that isn't quite perfect, or perfect for you, because you think it can be altered. The decision whether to buy the garment may depend upon your sewing experience, or whether you feel the garment requires a tailor's expertise, which would make the item more expensive. Is it worth it? It's usually not a split-second decision. If the alteration is minimal and if you're capable of sewing a seam, you're probably capable enough to shorten or lengthen a skirt, let out or take in a side seam, or put in a zipper. Why let your lack of confidence in doing alterations correctly force you to wear clothes that do not fit well or are unfashionable? Just take your time and attack the project carefully, but confidently.

Capability and sewing experience determine what alterations a woman

94

can do herself and what she'd be better off taking to a professional tailor. Very often the difference between what gets altered by a home sewer and what is given to a tailor is decided by the sewer's experience and by whether she has more time than money, or vice versa. Almost as often, the fabric is the deciding factor; the same sewer who tapers a linen coatdress herself will give a much thicker wool broadcloth coat to a tailor for tapering. Most of us don't feel capable to put a new zipper in our favorite suede pants or to taper an exquisite wool melton coat. Certain special-care fabrics (fur, suede, leather, metallics, sequins, and pile) deserve extra care and attention during alteration. If you're not familiar with their characteristics, refer to the fabric charts in Chapter 4 before you start sewing. You may pick up some helpful new information.

Some alterations don't even require a sewing machine. Hems always look better when they're made by hand; so do zippers. Small sewing details, like taking in a dart or removing a collar and refinishing the neckline also need not be done by machine. Generally these alterations look better when they're done by hand because hand sewing is characteristically less visible than machine sewing, partly because hand sewing can be spaced more widely than machine sewing.

HEMS

The simplest hemming mistakes are the ones most commonly made and easiest to avoid. We remember once (admittedly, long ago) measuring a skirt and then hemming it, only to find that we had marked the length carelessly and the skirt was too short. We hope the Salvation Army found a good home for it.

This mistake is easy to avoid. Measure and mark the final hem length with tailor's chalk or pins and try the garment on to make sure that the hem is all one length and that there is no sloping *before* you cut off any fabric. Wear the shoes you plan to wear with the garment.

Circular and *bias skirts* are two of the most difficult garments to hem. Because of all the fullness in a circular skirt, the fabric never seems to fall to the same length in any two places. This style requires a lot of time measuring and trying on the skirt to ensure that the hem is parallel and perpendicular to the floor throughout. A friend and a triple mirror are great assets here.

Bias skirts and dresses also tend to pose problems because the fabric will "give" and the hem will slope to one side. To minimize these problems,

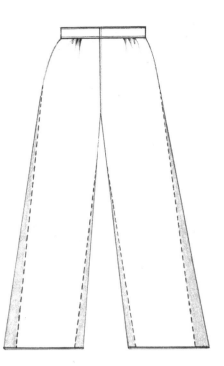

Taper your seams gradually when taking in a garment; otherwise your alteration will be the center of attention.

pin the skirt and baste in the hem. Then let the garment hang overnight. The next morning, check the garment for fabric sloping or irregularity before you finish it.

TAKING SEAMS IN

It's easy to make mistakes when you try to take seams in; it's almost as easy to avoid them by doing a little planning first, and by always fitting before you do anything drastic, like cutting or sewing.

When you take in a garment at the side or center seams, gradually taper the stitching so that your seams aren't deformed and don't stick out. If the tapering is abrupt, your skirt or dress will lose its smooth lines and your seams, which should be invisible, will be the center of attention and will tell the world that your garment was altered badly. Taper your seams gradually. Don't go overboard. If you're not careful, you'll change the lines of the garment, and you don't want to do that.

Remember your arithmetic, too. If you have to take in a skirt or dress 3″, either take in each side seam 1½″ or take in each side seam 1″ and take in the center back seam (assuming there is one) 1″. Otherwise you'll find you have moved your seams off center and distorted the lines of your garment.

MORE ABOUT SEAMS

Seams need *thread*—a little item that most sewers really don't know enough about. First let's look at color. Most of us have often fallen into the sloppy habit of choosing a *similar color* thread, rather than searching for the exact color. It can make a huge difference in the final look of your garment, so take a little extra time at the start, when you're mending or beginning a new sewing project, to select a thread that's *two shades darker* than the fabric you're working with. Thread on a spool often appears darker than it actually is, so lay a single thread over the fabric to make sure it's the right color.

Choose the type of thread according to the fabric you're working with:

SILK THREAD—Use for silk, silk blends, shiny wools, chiffon, batiste, fine
    laces, and voiles or rayons with a shiny finish.
MERCERIZED COTTON THREAD—Use for cotton, cotton blends, linen,
    rayon, man-made sheers.
SYNTHETIC (DACRON OR POLYESTER) THREAD—Use for synthetic fabrics
    and wool flannels, crêpe, chintz, faille, and other medium-weight
    fabrics.

After you've decided which thread is suitable for your fabric, it's time to choose your needle size and stitch length if you're sewing by machine. Here is a simple guide:

FINE FABRICS—For chiffon, silk gauze, sheers, and similar fabrics, use a
    setting between 15 and 20. Use a very fine needle (size 9) to
    avoid snagging the delicate threads of these sheer and fragile fabrics.
LIGHTWEIGHT FABRICS—Cotton batiste, velvets, fine corduroys, and
    similar fabrics require a stitch setting between 12 and 15 and a size
    11 needle.
MEDIUM-WEIGHT FABRICS—Piqué, faille, crêpes, and similar fabrics
    require a stitch setting between 10 and 12 and a needle size between
    14 and 16, depending on the weight and weave of the fabric.
HEAVYWEIGHT FABRICS—Gabardine, canvas, denim, ticking, and similar
    fabrics require a stitch setting between 8 and 10 and a needle size
    between 16 and 18, depending on the weight and weave of
    the fabric.

When you sew, pay special attention to curved seams. They'll come out perfectly if you use a shorter stitch length around the curves.

ZIPPERS

Zippers can look horrible if they've been put in carelessly. They can also enhance the look and quality of a garment if they've been put in well. That's why it often pays to remove a perfectly good machine-sewn zipper and then to sew it in, invisibly, by hand. We had a wonderful vintage skirt that we loved to wear for special occasions, but the zipper attracted more attention than the skirt's unusual flocked fabric. After we took out the zipper and put it in by hand, it was unnoticeable. Now the skirt's exquisite fabric and wonderful 1950s lampshade shape get all the attention.

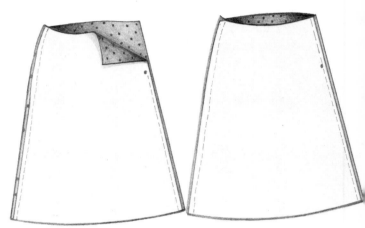

TO INSERT A ZIPPER BY HAND

1. *Remove existing zipper with care.*
2. *Baste zipper opening closed as though you were making a seam. Press open.*
3. *Position closed zipper, placing the pull tab ⅛ inch (3mm.) below the waistline or waistband. Align center of zipper with seam; baste in place.*
4. *Remove seam basting so you can open the zipper. Check to see that zipper placement is correct and that zipper opens and closes with ease.*
5. *Hand-sew securely and invisibly in place.*

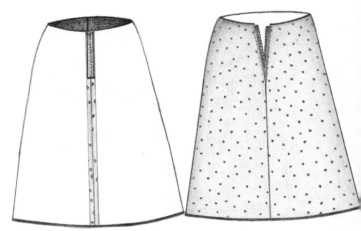

POCKETS

Pocket placement and size can affect not only the look and style of a garment, but can also accentuate personal figure problems. The two types of pockets that often require altering are the patch- and slash-pocket styles. We've all had the experience of trying on a beautiful pair of trousers of a straight skirt with slash pockets. Sadly enough, the pockets drew attention to our hips, and because they bulged, they made us look as though we were three months' pregnant.

Sometimes the solution to awkward and unflattering slash pockets is simply to pass up the garment; but if you're in love with it, you can usually remove the pockets and simply leave the slash-pocket look. There are two ways to do this: *to retain the slash-pocket look*, cut away most of the pocket, leaving only about 1″ or 2″ inside, and either pink, hem, or finish the edges of each pocket with seam binding, depending on the pocket's fabric. Or, if

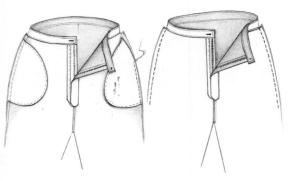

RETAIN THE SLASH-POCKET LOOK

ELIMINATE THE SLASH POCKET
IN SIDE SEAM

you prefer, you can sew the edges of the pocket together. The pockets will not be usable, but they won't bulge, either.

If the pocket fabric is very heavy, you may be better off *completely eliminating the slash pocket and its fashion detail*. Carefully rip out the pocket and completely close up the side seam, as though there had never been a pocket. We chose this option in altering a heavy linen skirt whose slash pockets were made of self-fabric, and immediately lost 2″ in our hip measurements when we wore the skirt.

Patch pockets must be positioned perfectly on blazers, skirts, and trousers. The placement and size can make the difference between a merely nice garment and a style statement. Often clothing which would have looked better without pockets is ruined because of the extra added designer detail. Don't be discouraged if you find a wonderful piece of clothing with awkwardly placed pockets. Removing them is one of the simplest alterations to do and can make an enormous difference in the garment's look.

Many fabrics (most wools, cottons, linens, and synthetics) will not show any marks when you remove patch pockets. However, on certain pile fabrics, like velvets, pocket removal can leave permanent stitching marks. If you plan to remove pockets from garments made of these fabrics, try removing a small area first and steaming or dry-ironing the fabric, depending upon the fiber content, to test whether the stitching marks can indeed be removed.

Some alterations aren't worth the effort, and you can save lots of time and money by avoiding potential mistakes. Generally, taking hems and cuffs up or down is an easy job. So is removing pockets. Altering a lining and taking in or letting out the sides of skirts or pants is harder. *Anything involving a pants crotch is trouble.* In fact, most alterations on pants can be trouble.

Weigh the price of the garment versus the alteration time and money required to put the garment into top shape. Sometimes it's better to pass up a good buy because it needs too much recutting to make the good buy a great outfit. Any large alteration job for which you question your ability may be the type of alteration to avoid. Tailors can be expensive. The time and money involved in drastic alterations generally makes them not worth all the effort and expense.

Realize when an alteration is just plain impossible, or impossible for you. Know your capabilities and know the amount of time you are willing to contribute to the altering of your garment. Some purchases are well worth that time. But for most others, you'll do yourself a big favor by passing up that "great buy." When you consider all the time and money the alterations will take, and the possibility that the alterations won't be completely successful, it probably isn't really such a great buy, after all.

Instead, since it's almost always easier to make a garment from scratch than to alter it, perhaps we can tempt you into making that beautiful garment yourself (see chapters 17 and 18). If we can't, we hope we can persuade you to keep on looking for something that won't have to be altered at all, or that will require only minor alterations.

Part three
SHOPPING

7
Shopping: Basic Strategy, Baroque Variations

SHOPPING CAN BE a chore, a bore, or an adventure. By developing a personal strategy, a woman who used to dread shopping can learn to enjoy it, and a woman who loves shopping can make the time she spends in stores more productive.

Whether or not you love to shop, happy, unexhausting shopping begins with good organization. It doesn't matter too much if you're just going to pick up some basics—underwear or a pair of sneakers. But if you're going to buy anything more serious or complicated, a little planning will save you lots of time and money. Making a list may sound silly to you: "Of course I know what I want to buy!" you snap. Until you remember that stores are in the business of delighting you, distracting you, and making you spend more time, and consequently more money, than you originally planned to.

So, we repeat, make a list of what you want to buy and what you want it to coordinate with. If you shop once a week, as many working women do, scan the newspaper ads the week before you shop to see whether any store is having a sale on what you need, or on something that could substitute for what you need, or on something you might need sometime this year. But *remember* that planning is great only when it's flexible. If you see a fantastic sale advertised, cancel your original plans and go to that sale. That's one of the best ways to save on your clothing budget and really stretch those dollars.

And bring the ads along; sometimes not all the sale merchandise has been reticketed, and you'll need the ad to prove your point.

BASIC GEOGRAPHY

One of the greatest savers of your time and money is a knowledge of the layout of your favorite two or three stores. By the time you've lived somewhere for six months or a year, you've probably found two or three stores where you prefer to shop, where you like the merchandise, prices, and service. You've probably even narrowed down your choice to specific departments in those stores. Whenever you shop, you'll save a lot of time and money by going to those departments first—and to the sales racks in those departments.

Let's make this technique more concrete with a specific example. At Alexander's branch at Lexington Avenue and 58th Street, our favorite New York City store for basic shopping, there are two major sale-rack areas that are always our first—and often our only—stop. These are the areas where the hottest sale merchandise is displayed, where we think the best bargains are. One area is on the main floor, just before the escalators. The second area is on the second floor in the front of the store, and includes the clearance rack and several special designer sales racks with many one-of-a-kind items. In less than a half hour, we can "case" Alexander's and pick up any bargains that grab us. For us, this zip-in, zip-out shopping ploy gives us a great return on the time we invest.

This method isn't one hundred percent infallible, although it's pretty close. Stores will rearrange sales areas seasonally, and will sometimes completely redo whole floors or the entire store. But these changes are easy for frequent shoppers to spot and are easily taken in stride.

WHAT TO WEAR FOR SHOPPING

If you want to match a particular garment, wear it. If it's too bulky, dressy, or unsuitable for street and shopping wear, carry it in a tote. Pulling a thread from the hem or seam allowance just won't work; threads are so small that they blend into whatever you place them against. And, unless you know you have a superb memory for colors (or live just around the corner and don't mind returning or exchanging things), don't rely on your memory.

Also in the tote should go the shoes you'll be wearing with what you plan to buy. Wear comfortable shoes, even if they're sneakers, especially if you're going to spend all day shopping. Don't forget a tape measure and your wardrobe inventory.

The best outfit to wear for shopping is two neutral-colored pieces. A sweater with a V neck or a back zipper is especially good because it won't muss up your hair even after many try-ons. A shirt or blouse without too many buttons is another good choice. Your skirt or pants should be easy to get in and out of, too. Few things are more frustrating than struggling in and out of tight jeans—fraying tempers and breaking nails in the process.

If you're trying on clothes in a store or factory showroom or outlet without dressing rooms, you'll have to dress differently. Under these exposed conditions, the best outfit to wear is leotard-based, so that you can try on clothes in public without sacrificing your modesty. A light-colored leotard and a voluminous skirt is a pretty combination, which will let you try on tops over the leotard, which creates minimum bulk and distortion, and slip on pants and skirts under your skirt. Dresses are a little trickier, but can be tried on over the head, after which the skirt is slipped off underneath. Usually the bargains obtainable in places without dressing rooms make this hassle worthwhile.

SAVE TIME ON TRY-ONS

Don't exhaust yourself trying on anything until you've measured it. Measure tops at the underarm, being careful not to stretch knits. Skirts and pants should be measured at the waist and hips (in most designs, 7″–8″ below the waist). Ignore size markings. We consider ourselves average; yet, according to assorted designers—and, in some cases, the same designer—we wear any size between 6 (some skirts) and large (some tops). We'll try on anything, regardless of size, especially if it's on sale. You should do the same.

ALL ABOUT LABELS

Have you ever wondered how designers like Calvin Klein, Anne Klein, Bill Blass, and Geoffrey Beene can manage to design everything from jeans to linens and bedding, to cosmetics, to sunglasses, to clothes for the entire family?

Designers license their names for use on products. These products—jeans are a good example—generally sell much better with the designer label, and thus make the licensing business venture profitable for both the designers and their licensees. Depending on the specific business agreement, the designers (or their companies) will receive a great deal of money for their participation in the creation of the product and for the use of their names—a great status symbol for many consumers.

Very often, though, the only "designer" feature in the licensed garment is the designer label. Designers may have very little to do with the creation, colors, style, fit, and quality of the product. It all depends upon the degree to which designers wish to get involved. They may merely give the final approval to the fit of a pair of jeans. Or they may get very involved in creating a new color palette for their active-sportswear licensees, or the designing of a new motif and look for their bed-linen licensees. Their involvement depends upon the amount of time they are able to spend, and generally there's never enough time, especially when they have to think about their scarf, shoe, sheet, towel, hosiery, sportswear, and designer collections all at once!

Designers do not have day-to-day control of quality and business procedures over their licensees; sometimes they are the last to see the final product. It is essential that designers deal only with good and reputable manufacturers who will deliver quality products which will deserve the designer's name.

When you see a Bill Blass, Mary McFadden, or Oscar de la Renta label in the bed-and-bath department or the junior sportswear department, as in *Name of Designer* for *Name of Linen Company*, you can bet that it's a licensing arrangement. It's not a "real" designer label, in which the designer's name stands alone. A designer's label tells us that the designer was involved in the creation, fabric selection, tailoring, finishing, and final look of the garment. This careful attention to every step of the garment's design and manufacture often requires total involvement in the evolution of a style or a look. Licensing is really a business venture. While designers usually create the garment, design motifs for fabrics, or choose color palettes, they are much less concerned with the licensees' products than with their own lines, which represent a certain degree of quality and creativity. They know that their reputations are riding on their own expensive fashions, not on their licensees' garments.

IS THE GARMENT REALLY WORTH THE PRICE?

Okay, you've tried on the sweater, blouse, dress, pants, or skirt, and you look marvelous. You're even thinking of buying it. But is it really a good buy? Is it worth it? Three factors will help you determine its real cost: initial cost, upkeep, and cost per wearing.

The *initial cost* is the garment's price. Sales can be deceptive here. Markdowns (see Chapter 9) can be seductive, especially if your beautiful buy is only $150, marked down from $400. Stop and think for a couple of minutes. Pretend that it was never marked down and that $150 is the original price. Is it worth $150 to you?

Upkeep is another important factor. How often will the garment need cleaning? Is it hand- or machine-washable, or will it have to go to the cleaner's? If your garment needs cleaning every time it's worn, and you wear it often, at $2.00 per cleaning you can easily pay in cleaning bills what the garment originally cost.

Cost per wearing is based on initial cost plus upkeep. It works like this: if you buy something for $50 and you wear it twenty times a year for five years, its initial cost is 50 cents cents per wearing (one hundred wearings for $50). If it has to be cleaned every five wearings and costs $2.00 per cleaning, add 40 cents per wearing for the cleaning, to arrive at a cost of 90 cents per wearing. (This cost per wearing can be almost halved by using bulk dry-cleaning machines or hand-washing.)

There's another way to look at costs, too. When you're trying to decide between a $50 garment and a cheaper version for $35, ask yourself:

Is 75 cents or $1.00 per wearing really so much money if it provides much better quality, looks, and feel than 50 cents or 70 cents per wearing?
Is the cheaper garment really cheaper if it lasts only a year ($35 per year) and the more expensive garment lasts two years ($25 per year)?
Since the cheap garment will have to be replaced much sooner, and its replacement will cost more because of inflation, won't this choice really *cost more* than the more expensive garment would have in the first place?

If your shopping choices have passed all the acid tests (remember the chapters on fabric, tailoring, and alterations), here's a way to stretch your money further by delaying the billing on your purchases.

CREDIT-CARD STRATEGY

If you can find banks that are still issuing free credit cards by the time you read this, here's a wonderful way to get almost two months' free credit on anything you buy:

Let's assume that you have two MasterCards, whose billing dates are the 7th and 21st of each month and two VISA cards, whose billing dates are the 15th and 30th of each month. Stick little gummed labels showing the billing date on each card, or write the date on the signature strip of the card.

Any purchase that's billed on the first MasterCard from September 5 won't be processed in time for the September 7 bill; it will appear on the October 7 bill, and you'll have until early November to pay for it.

Accordingly, you can rotate your four credit cards this way to obtain maximum interest-free credit:

MasterCard billing date 7th of month—use between the 5th and the 12th of the month. Then switch to

VISA billing date 15th of month—use between the 13th and the 18th of the month. Then switch to

MasterCard billing date 21st of month—use between the 19th and the 27th of the month. Then switch to

VISA billing date 30th of month—use between the 28th and the 4th of the next month.

And so on and so forth.

Be prepared to pay off the entire bill before the due date, or this strategy won't work and you may have to pay some horrendous interest charges.

KEEPING TRACK OF YOUR BILLS

It's a good idea to keep all your monthly charge slips in an envelope and to take them with you when you shop. Or you can keep notes of how much you spent, where, and for what in a small pocket notebook. Keeping track of your expenses has several advantages. You'll be able to check your bills against your charge slips to make sure there are no errors. (Computers may not make mistakes, but their operators sure do!) Even better, you'll be able to keep an eye on your expenses. If you've splurged one month (for something wonderful, of course), you'll want to curb your extravagances for the next month or two. And this brings us to

YOUR CLOTHING BUDGET

We're not compulsive budgeters, but we do recognize the value of a budget, and we do earmark money for periodic clothing sales. You should do likewise. If possible, set aside at least 50 percent of your clothing budget, or be willing to borrow, if necessary, for the annual January sales. Even if it costs 18 or 20 percent a year to borrow money, it's well worth it if you can save from 50 to 80 percent. And if you pay off the loan in three months, it will cost you no more than 5 percent.

The January sales offer not only the best fall/winter merchandise, but also luxury clothing items that weren't sold at Christmas. Designer boutiques hold marvelous January sales, too. Hunt around in them as well as in the major department stores. (We bought a beautiful cabled cashmere cardigan at Hermès one January, marked down from $200 to $50.)

So much for shopping hints and strategies. We think of browsing as something apart from shopping—a sort of baroque variation on the basic technique.

BROWSING

Browsing covers a lot of ground: shopping without a specific item in mind, investigating a new store or department, checking out a clearance sale, or merchandise shortly before you think it will be put on sale. When we browse systematically—even one lunch hour a week—browsing is a more enjoyable and considerably less expensive method of building a wardrobe than going to major department stores and buying a seasonal wardrobe all at once.

Browsing doesn't require money, although perhaps you should be prepared to buy something really outstanding. When you browse, you're just looking around, taking mental notes, and occasionally trying on some promising selections.

Browsing and shopping piecemeal require creativity, as well as a thorough knowledge of what you already own. Here's where your wardrobe inventory in a notebook comes in handy. If you have a list of all the skirts and pants you own, you know whether that fabulous sweater will turn out to be a buy or a bomb.

The true creativity and fun of browsing and shopping this way is that it is a way to expand your wardrobe with things you love, not clothes you think you need. After all, there is very little we really *need* in our wardrobes. After those basics have been acquired, we express our personal taste and love of good things. Looking in many stores gives you the greatest opportunity to fill out and expand your wardrobe with a wide variety of interesting clothes. It also keeps you aware of what is succeeding and what is failing each season —an interesting side benefit. A clearance rack full of mandarin-collared tunics may seem like a great buy, but if you see them on clearance racks in every store, either no one liked them well enough to buy them, or they're defective or poorly designed. Unless they suit you unusually well and you're certain that they're not damaged, you're better off without them, too.

Browsing can also teach you about pattern sizing. Some designers' clothes will almost always look well on you; some will almost always look horrendous. A good part of this is due to the way in which designers size their patterns. Some designers have bean poles in mind; others think more realistically of the way most women are built. After you try on a number of designers' clothes, you'll know not only what flatters you and what's impossible, but also what size you wear in a specific designer's line. This knowledge will save you a lot of time later on, when you're deciding what to try on.

When you browse, don't forget to check departments besides the ones in which you usually shop. Men's and boys' departments are wonderful sources for sweaters, shirts, and sometimes even jackets. We've found some of our best, most beautifully made shirts—at bargain prices, of course—in men's departments. Junior and teen departments are prime sources for small women. (See Chapter 8 for more hints for petite sizes.)

Best of all, browsing will help you identify which stores are best for you: for your wardrobe needs, your life-style, your budget. By screening stores and getting quick overviews of their merchandise, sale, and return policies, you'll be able to find the best stores for your size, style, time schedule, and purse.

8
Special Sizes— *Not* *Special Problems*

WHEN WE WERE asked to write this chapter, we didn't feel that large women and petites had special problems finding attractive clothes. After all, while researching other chapters of this book, we had found clothes racks in store after store marked "Size 2-20," "Size 4-18." Now, after even more research, we still feel the same way. Five or ten years ago, very large and very small women had problems finding appropriate, attractive clothes. Large women often wound up looking worse than matronly; small women looked like dolls or like little girls.

But times have changed. Let's look at the small sizes first.

When one-piece, defined-waistline, heavily darted dresses went out of fashion and soft "separates" dressing came in, most fashion problems for petite women vanished. Just being able to buy and wear a separate skirt meant that the waist fit and was placed correctly, automatically. The hem could always be taken up a couple of inches. And as long as the top was tucked in, or could be hemmed easily, it really didn't matter how long it was. In most garments, the shoulder seams were in the right places and the sleeves were the right length, or could be hemmed or tucked.

Another fashion change which eliminated problems for petite women was simply the manufacture of garments in smaller sizes. Virtually all designers make size 4, which is scaled down properly to be smaller all over, not just in length. Size 2 is becoming more common, and many stores around the country specialize in junior sizes 1-3-5. Clothing designers, manufacturers, and retail stores have finally realized that thirty-three million women are 5'4" and under, and they all want to profit from this lucrative market.

Finally, one fashion change over the past five or ten years is so obvious that most people—other than fashion historians—don't even notice it. Like many periods in history (but unlike 1900 to 1960), children are wearing scaled-down versions of their parents' clothes. This means that a tiny woman can wear a girl's size 12 and 14 clothes without looking silly. Many women's designers do a children's line now, too. Very small women can buy an Anne Klein suit in a girl's size 14, or Calvin Klein and Ralph Lauren separates for girls. All they're missing is the high price tag. Our petite friend Cindi, who teaches law at Loyola University, shopped with us and found two identical blouses by Gunne Sax. The woman's size 6 cost $40; the girl's size 14 cost $28. Guess which one Cindi bought!

And, of course, small women who want to dress in the "preppie" style can buy beautifully tailored clothes in boys' departments.

We see so many clothes in size 4—even in middle-of-the-road and budget stores—that we don't feel small women have clothing problems anymore. There's only one garment we can think of that might be difficult to find: an evening dress. If you're petite and lead the kind of social life that demands formal evening clothes, you're best off making your own. Even if you're not an experienced sewer, you should find the designs in chapters 17 and 18 easy to make and not too time consuming. Remember that simplicity of design is what makes evening clothes elegant, instead of busy.

Pat Swift, president of Plus Model Management Ltd., a modeling agency that specializes in large and small sizes, suggests that petite women:

> Never wear skirts longer than 1" below your knee. This hemline will give you the most attractive proportions and will make you look taller.
>
> Long sleeves should end just at the wristbone. If they're shorter, you'll look as though you're wearing your daughter's clothes; if they're longer, you'll look as though you're trying to grow into an outfit that's much too big for you. In sleeve lengths, a mere ½" can make or break a look.
>
> Don't use sharp color breaks or contrasts at the waist. Give the illusion of one beautiful long line with subtle, monochromatic colors and textures. You can use color contrasts away from your waist—in your jewelry, shoes, and purse.

Never wear more than a 2″ heel in an effort to appear taller. The heel-
height/leg-length proportion becomes overbalanced, and you'll
look as though you're on stilts.

Good posture will make you look not only taller, but also more powerful.
This is very important for petite women executives.

Buy shirts, blazers, and jackets in boys' departments. The tailoring and
fabric offer great value at reasonable prices.

Big women, too, no longer have problems finding attractive clothes in
all sizes and price ranges. Clothing designers and manufacturers finally took
out their little pocket calculators, punched in some numbers, and realized
that if the thirty million women who wear size 14 and larger each spent only
$100 a year on clothes, this was a $3 billion market! That's why we're suddenly seeing designer jeans, silk shirts and shirtwaists, and elegantly tailored
suits in large sizes. When the work of Cardin, Givenchy, Harvé Benard,
Joseph Picone, Chaus, and The Right Honourable Company of Silk Mer-
chants can be found in women's departments, big women have no excuse to
be frumpy.

Of course, there's a difference between a size 14 (considered a large size
by the high-fashion designers, some of whom now stop at a size 10) and a
size 20, a size 16½, and a size 48. And it's still true that the larger you are,
the less choice you'll have in finding pretty clothes. But the important point
is that now size 16s, 18s, and 20s and the smaller half sizes and women's sizes
can find beautiful clothes.

Now there's even a fashion and beauty magazine for big women:

Big Beautiful Woman
3518 Cahuenga Boulevard West
Suite 210
Los Angeles, CA 90068

Most department stores now have large-size departments, usually easily
identified by name, like Women's World. For example: Macy's Big City
Woman and Lord Taylor's 12/20 Shop. Lane Bryant and Roaman's have
branches all over the country; some cities even have four or five branches. But
if you've just moved to a new city or town, or just gained a lot of weight and
don't know where to look first for pretty, large-size clothes, write to some of
the designers who make your favorite styles and ask which stores in your
area carry their garments in your size. (Addresses of some popular large-size
designers are listed later in this chapter.)

Don't forget men's departments, either. For many broad-shouldered, long-armed, long-legged women—regardless of size—men's clothes fit better than women's. They're also *always* better constructed and tailored, and are usually made of better fabric. For large women, men's shirts and sweaters will almost always fit better than women's; and if the shirts have a center placket, rather than just an overlap, no one more than six inches away from you will be able to tell which way they button. And, for large women, men's slacks may sometimes fit better than women's. Certainly, the fabric selection will be greater.

Pat Swift, the "perfect size 16" president of Plus Model Management, has some advice for large women, based on her own experience and that of her models:

"Don't put off buying attractive clothes now because you think you may go on a diet. Buy some nice clothes now and look as pretty as you can—hair, makeup, the works. If you invest in a complete wardrobe, stabilize your size and weight. Make it anything you feel comfortable with, but do stabilize your weight within five to eight pounds. Otherwise, you'll keep on growing in and out of your clothes, and you'll only frustrate yourself. Shelley Winters, who often has to gain and lose weight for her acting roles, has a complete wardrobe in sizes 8 to 18, so that no matter what she weighs, she's always beautifully dressed. But, since most of us can't afford complete wardrobes in five or six different sizes, we have to keep our weight within one size, or at most two."

Pat also suggests keeping color and accessory accents—scarves and jewelry—near the face, and letting your makeup be in proportion to your body. This means that you can wear false eyelashes that your smaller sisters could never get away with. Shoes and boots should be in proportion, too—high heels and dark-tinted stockings can be marvelously slimming.

Like petite women, about the only problem you may have is formal evening clothes. Our advice is almost the same: learn to sew simple fashions yourself (see chapters 17 and 18), or write to designer Sharon Rothfeld, who specializes in beautiful evening clothes for big women, to ask which stores in your area stock her clothes:

Sharon Rothfeld's New York
566 Seventh Avenue
New York, NY 10018

Here are some other designers who are doing collections for large women:

PAGE 116: *Beautiful clothes—from bathing suits and lingerie to evening dresses—are now available in large sizes to please the thirty million women who wear size 14 and up.* (PHOTO COURTESY PLUS MODELS LTD.)

Alfred Angelo, Inc.
1385 Broadway
New York, NY 10018

Chaus Inc.
1410 Broadway
New York, NY 10018

Givenchy Sport
1407 Broadway
New York, NY 10018

Harvé Benard
205 West 39th Street
New York, NY 10018

Ingrid Cado, Inc.
226 West 37th Street
New York, NY 10018

Joseph Picone Collections
1407 Broadway
New York, NY 10018

Leslie Fay, Inc.
1400 Broadway
New York, NY 10018

Lloyd Williams
1410 Broadway
New York, NY 10018

Pierre Cardin
1411 Broadway
New York, NY 10018

And here are some stores and factory outlets, besides Lane Bryant and Roaman's that specialize in large sizes. (We haven't included the smaller sizes because we feel that petite women don't have as much trouble finding clothes, thanks to separates dressing.)

ARIZONA

CAMELBACK

Lynn's
5033 North Central Avenue

PHOENIX

Bebe's Family Tree
2615 West Bethany Home Road

Clothing City
1600 South 16th Street

Pauline's Sportswear of California
7823 North 27th Avenue

TEMPE

Super Gal
6465 South Rural Road

CALIFORNIA

CHULA VISTA

Lady L Fashions
207 Third

Pretty & Plump Ladies Wear
542 Broadway

DALY CITY

Fern Warner
7 Westlake Mall

EL CAJON

Little Extra Fashions
330 Broadway

Pretty & Plump Ladies Wear
450 Fletcher Parkway

ESCONDIDO

McCarty's
132 East Grand Avenue

Pretty & Plump Ladies Wear
119 East Grand Avenue

LA MESA

Pretty & Plump Ladies Wear
8333 La Mesa Boulevard

LOS ANGELES

Decade 80 Ladies Boutique
4367 South Western Avenue

Designers at Large
860 South Los Angeles Street

The Original Large and Half-Size
Factory Outlet
847 Santee Street

OCEANSIDE

Pretty & Plump Ladies Wear
1018 Mission Avenue

RICHMOND

Jerri B Large Sizes
Hilltop Shopping Center

SAN ANSELMO

Lusty Ladies
137 Tunstead Avenue

SAN BERNARDINO

The Original Large and Half-Size
Factory Outlet
663 West Second Street

SAN DIEGO

Big 'n' Beautiful Sportswear
3070 University Avenue

Jerome's Ladies Apparel
2930 University Avenue

SAN FRANCISCO

Fran's Apparel
1539 Fillmore

Marian's
2040 Mission

SAN RAFAEL

BG's Boutique
888 Fourth

Big & Beautiful
3815 Redwood Highway

VAN NUYS

The Original Large and Half-Size
Factory Outlet
6586 Van Nuys Boulevard

VISTA

Pauline's Fashions
854 South Santa Fe Avenue

COLORADO

DENVER

Catherine's Stout Shoppe
3311 East First Avenue
9797 West Colfax Avenue

Fashion Plus
4628 South Broadway
8440 West Colfax Avenue

Thelma's Place
2223 South Monaco

FLORIDA

JACKSONVILLE

Broadway Department Store
119 Broad

Catherine's Stout Shoppe
3500 Beach Boulevard
5501 Norwood Avenue

Slenderella Stout Shops
1048 Arlington Road
740 Edgewood
Gateway Shopping Center
237 North Laura Street
1011 Park Street
1966 San Marco Boulevard

MIAMI BEACH

Penny's Place, Inc.
227 71st Street

NORTH MIAMI

Half Sizes by Wendy's Place
2172 NE 123rd Street

SURFSIDE

First Lady
9551 Harding Avenue

GEORGIA

DECATUR

G's Ladies Apparel
1707 Church Street

ILLINOIS

CHICAGO

Central Specialty Shoppe
4342 North Central Avenue

Therese, Inc.
70 East Oak Street

KENTUCKY

LOUISVILLE

Catherine's Stout Shoppe
3002 Bardstown Road
4600 Shelbyville Road

Pretty Plus
McMahan Plaza
Hikes and Breckinridge

Women's World Shops
Jefferson Mall

LOUISIANA

GRETNA

Rosie's Youthful Stouts
558 Lapalco Boulevard

Sabrina's Stout Fashions
601 Terry Parkway

HARAHAN

Laurie-Linda Limited
6226 Jefferson Highway

METAIRIE

Catherine's Stout Shoppe
321 Causeway Boulevard

Evelyn's Women's Apparel
Clearview Shopping Center
Lakeside Shopping Center

Rosie's Youthful Stouts
2047 Metairie Road

NEW ORLEANS

Beatrice Shop Inc.
8127 Oak

Catherine's Stout Shoppe
3049 Gentilly Boulevard

The Vogue
1701 Dryades

MARYLAND
(AND WASHINGTON, D.C.)

BALTIMORE

Sixteen Plus Shop
North Plaza Mall

BETHESDA

Fashion Tree
    Wildwood Manor Center
    10231 Old Georgetown Road

OLNEY

Fashion Tree
    Olney Village Mart
    18220 Village Mart Drive

RANDALLSTOWN

Lovely Large Lady
8115 Liberty Road

MASSACHUSETTS

FALL RIVER

Fashion Factory Store
Weaver and West Streets

Linjay Manufacturing Corporation
1567 North Main Street

Robyn Wholesale Outlet
1567 North Main Street

MICHIGAN

LINCOLN PARK

Merry Widow
3406 Fort

OAK PARK

Special People
25250 Greenfield

RIVER ROUGE

Lee Ann's Dress Shop
228 Burke

MINNESOTA

COON RAPIDS

More to Love
2891 Coon Rapids Boulevard

MINNEAPOLIS

House of Large Sizes
    9 branches

Special Size Shop
    6215 Brooklyn Boulevard
    5034 France Avenue South
    45 South Seventh Street

MISSOURI

KANSAS CITY

Dubarry's
Metcalf South

Fashions at Large
9566 Quivira Road

House of Large Sizes
    5312 Chouteau
    4921 Johnson Drive
    4601 State
    7628 State

More Woman
2070 Independence Center
1124 West 103rd

ST. LOUIS

Just for You Ltd.
43 National Way Shopping Center
(141st & Manchester)

NEBRASKA

COUNCIL BLUFFS

Fashions at Large
2201 West Broadway

OMAHA

Catherine's Stout Shoppes
314 South 72nd
13447 West Center Road

Fashions at Large
2230 North 91 Plaza
8544 Park Drive

NEW JERSEY

BURLINGTON

Peerless Manufacturing Co. Factory
    Store
600 Jacksonville Road

CARLSTADT

Herald House
394 Veterans Boulevard

CLIFFSIDE PARK

Ilene James Sportswear
229 Walker Street

FLEMINGTON

Ladies Factory Outlet
Flemington Circle Park

GARFIELD

Irwin's Place
102 Somerset Street

JERSEY CITY

Bargain Bazaar
656 Newark Avenue

Fire Islander Factory Outlet
111 Port Jersey Boulevard

Smart Size (division of Lane Bryant)
2875 Kennedy Boulevard

NEWARK

Smart Size (division of Lane Bryant)
790 Broad Street

PASSAIC

R & S Garment, Inc. Factory Outlet
276 Passaic Avenue
    (closed summers)

PERTH AMBOY

Smart Size (division of Lane Bryant)
165 Smith Street

SADDLE BROOK

Sizes Unlimited (division of
    Roaman's)
250 Market Street

Smart Size (division of Lane Bryant)
Saddle Brook Mall

SECAUCUS

Abe Schrader Factory Outlet
Hartz Way

Wilroy Factory Outlet
111 Secaucus Road

SPRING LAKE

Sample House Manufacturers Outlet
524 Brighton Plaza

NEW YORK

HUNTINGTON (L.I.)

Printogs Factory Outlet II
394A New York Avenue

NEW YORK CITY

Alexander's Women's World
58th Street and Lexington Avenue

Ashanti
872 Lexington Avenue

Forgotten Woman
880 Lexington Avenue

Irving Katz
228 West 38th Street

Lord & Taylor 12/20 Shop
38th Street and Fifth Avenue

Macy's Big City Woman
34th Street and Broadway

Miss Cindee Modes
270 West 38th Street

Ms., Miss & Mrs.
462 Seventh Avenue

National Ladies' Specialty Shop
470 Seventh Avenue

Smart Size
111 East Fordham Road
Bronx

1360 Fulton Street
Brooklyn

Zynn Fashions (coats and suits)
270 West 38th Street
(by appointment only)

VALLEY STREAM (L.I.)

Smart Size
Green Acres Shopping Center

VICTOR

The 800 Shop
Eastview Park

WANTAGH (L.I.)

Marie's Fashion (factory outlet)
3270 Merrick Road

WEST SENECA

Fran Roberts Ltd.
Garden Village Plaza

OHIO

CINCINNATI

Butterfly Inc.
415 Wyoming Avenue

Elegance in a Woman's World
6654 Chestnut

CLEVELAND

Ashley's Inc.
4733 Great Northern

Something Extra
4487 Mayfield Road

PENNSYLVANIA

BERWYN

Lady Phillips
10 Leopard Road

BRISTOL

Importers Outlet
201 Basin Street

PHILADELPHIA

Brecher's Dress Shop
609 South Fourth Street

Larry's
2310 Chestnut

M&M Factory Store
707 West Grange Street

The Plus Woman
  1703 Walnut Street
  77th and City Line Avenue
  Jenkintown Square (lower level)

Shelley Shoppe
6609 Castor Avenue

Sixteen Plus
Rising Sun Plaza

PITTSBURGH

The Belladonna
2893 West Liberty Avenue

PLEASANT HILLS

Joanne Stout Shops
589 Clairton Boulevard

TENNESSEE

COLLIERVILLE

Pat's Stout Shop
626 Chaney Drive

MADISON

Catherine's Stout Shoppe
1206 Gallatin Road South

MEMPHIS

Catherine's Stout Shoppes
  4279 Highway 51S
  64 Main Street
  541 Perkins Street Ext.
  1992 Union Avenue

Friedman's Fashions
57 North Main

NASHVILLE

Catherine's Stout Shoppe
  4092 Hillsboro Road

Forever Young Stout Shops
  1767 Gallatin Road
  5326 Hickory Hollow Parkway
  3730 Old Hickory Boulevard

TEXAS

DALLAS

Manufacturers Sample Outlet
  1306 Inwood Road
  2476 West Illinois

My Lady
Carillon Plaza

Sledge's Stylish Stout Shops
  320 Inwood Village
  6110 Luther Lane
  730 Wynnewood Village

Toy Wynn Fashions for the Fuller
  Figure
1214 Preston Royal Plaza

FORT WORTH

Sledge's Stylish Stout Shops
5288 Trail Lake Drive

HOUSTON

Carroll's Fashions
10 Woodlake Square

The Woman's Shop
  219 Gulfgate Mall
  748 Memorial City
  214 Northline Mall
  2427 South Post Oak Road

SAN ANTONIO

Capri II
155 East Houston Street

Lady Mignon Plus Sizes
4119 McCullough

WASHINGTON

BELLEVUE

Queen Size Boutique
2102 140th NE

NORTH END

Chubby & Tubby
7906 Aurora North

SEATTLE

Queen Size Boutique
4530 University Village Court NE

SOUTH END

Chubby & Tubby
3333 Rainier South

WHITE CENTER

Chubby & Tubby
9456 16th SW

WASHINGTON, D.C.

(See Maryland)

WISCONSIN

MILWAUKEE

Fashions at Large
    13420 Watertown Plank Road
    130 West Silver Spring Drive

Sizes Unlimited
    2335 North 124th
    5491 South 76th
    8159 West Brown Deer Road

9

Clearance as a Way of Life,

OR IT ISN'T A BARGAIN UNLESS IT'S MARKED DOWN AT LEAST 50 PERCENT

ONE OF OUR FRIENDS took the Eastern Airlines shuttle to Boston very early one August morning to get to Filene's Basement at 9 A.M. for the annual designer fur sale. She bought a full-length ranch mink coat and a Russian squirrel jacket with a fox-trimmed hood, and made it back to New York in time for a three o'clock editorial meeting. Even after her plane ticket and cab fares, *she saved $6,000 over the retail price of the furs!*

Being a truly dedicated bargain hunter is partly an art and partly a science. It means outguessing both the store and other shoppers. Clearance racks are like Chinese auctions, where the prices on whatever merchandise remains are reduced periodically. You want to get those buys at the lowest possible price, but not to miss out on them and lose the bargains to another demon shopper. For example, right now we've got our eye on a cashmere bathrobe on sale for $55 at our favorite sweater factory. (It's $195 at Bloomingdale's and Bergdorf Goodman.) But, since it's an extravagance and we'd like to pay only $40, we're going to check back the day after Thanksgiving. If it's still there and marked down, we'll take it. If it's gone, maybe there will be another one on the sale rack just after Christmas.

126

BROWSING HELPS HERE

Browsing (see Chapter 7) is one good way to begin clearance shopping. If you browse certain stores on a fairly regular basis, you'll get a pretty clear idea of what merchandise is moving quickly and what merchandise seems almost welded to the rack, week after week. If the clothes you love are moving very slowly, it's a good bet that they'll be marked down sooner or later.

Once the merchandise is marked down, browsing can help you pinpoint the optimum time to buy. If there are only one or two of a garment that you like and the price is right, grab it when you see it at the first markdown. But if there are dozens, it's pretty safe to wait a week or two—checking the racks once or twice in the meantime—to see if your choice will be marked down again. In fact, each time you check the racks and sales tables, there will probably be new merchandise for you to make a mental note about.

FILENE'S BASEMENT

Our rules for shopping at Filene's Basement differ from all the hints and advice given earlier. There are two related reasons for this: First, we've never been able to spend more than three or four days at a time in Boston, so we can't visit Filene's more than twice during any one trip. Second, there are so many other dedicated bargain hunters in Filene's Basement that choices must be immediate and firm. You can't shilly-shally when half a dozen women are waiting for you to hang up that beautiful bargain so they can snatch it off the rack and try it on. Our philosophy is to buy, even when in minor doubt, because we know it's really a once-in-a-lifetime shot. Since the merchandise is returnable, we know we can always try it on in our hotel room and return it if it's really a disaster.

There's only one basic problem in shopping in Filene's Basement: there are no dressing rooms, so all merchandise must be tried on in full view of all the other shoppers and browsers, some of whom will surely be men. (They're not necessarily voyeurs; they may be shopping with their wives or girl friends.) To protect ourselves, we've evolved the Filene's-Basement-trying-on-outfit: the light-colored leotard (sleeveless in summer, long-sleeved in winter) and tights and a full skirt we described earlier.

Filene's Basement is one place where measuring garments before trying them on is a necessity. *Don't forget your tape measure, and do keep it handy, so that you won't have to keep groping for it.*

With all the hassles involved in trying on clothes right on the sales floor of Filene's Basement, we love it, make it our first stop on every trip to Boston, and rate it as our favorite store in the United States for these reasons:

The salespeople are extraordinarily helpful and courteous, especially under difficult circumstances, like being avalanched by customers on sale days and having to cope with tons of merchandise being thrown around by bargain hunters, who almost never put things back where they found them.

Our fellow customers are friendly and helpful. There's a sorority-house feeling at Filene's Basement. Women take turns zipping and unzipping each other, trying on one-of-a-kind designer clothes, for which a waiting line may develop, sharing mirrors, and acting as friendly critics—even for total strangers. We've never seen any pushing, elbowing, umbrellas-deployed-as-strategic-weapons at even the biggest Filene's sales.

Finally, the fantastic bargains. Filene's gets some of its best merchandise at the end of the season, from such stores as I. Magnin, Neiman-Marcus, Bergdorf Goodman, Bloomingdale's, Lord and Taylor, Sakowitz, and even Holt Renfrew in Canada. Not only are the clothes marked down enormously from the original price, to begin with, but under Filene's automatic markdown policy, the prices are reduced another 25 percent after twelve selling days, an additional 25 percent after six more days, and another 25 percent after six more selling days, for a total markdown of 75 percent after twenty-four selling days. (After thirty selling days, unsold merchandise is donated to charity and generally winds up at the Goodwill store on Berkeley Street in downtown Boston.) The "entry day" is marked clearly on the sales ticket, so that customers can request additional markdowns if the garment has somehow evaded Filene's sharp pencils.

For example, a $600 evening dress from Neiman-Marcus might be ticketed at $159.95 when it first came into Filene's Basement. After twelve selling days, if it was still on the racks, it would be marked down to $119.95. After eighteen selling days, the dress would be marked $79.95, and, finally, after twenty-four selling days, the dress would be marked $39.95. Of course, most great buys are grabbed immediately, or no later than the first markdown. Some of the wonderful things we've bought at Filene's Basement over the years are:

A Halston peach Ultrasuede jacket—originally $200—for $40. It's seven
   years old, and we wear it nearly every day in the spring and early
   summer.
A Holly's Harp printed scarlet silk décolleté cocktail or short evening
   dress—originally $755—for $89.95.
A Basile four-piece gray and beige tweed suit (jacket, skirt, blouse, and
   tunic)—originally $700—for $89.95. All the pieces work well
   separately, with other skirts, blouses, and dresses, as well as together.
A Valentino white wool gabardine jacket—originally $300—for $60. It
   turns our white wool gabardine skirt and pants into suits. Originally
   worn only for spring, these outfits really got a workout when the
   black-and-white look was so popular.

Because these designer clothes are last season's or last year's, are Filene's
bargain hunters doomed to looking passé? Pat Patricelli, the publicity director
of Filene's, doesn't think so. In fact, she says, "Many of the clothes we get in
the Basement store were so avant-garde that they didn't sell in their local
stores. The women were too conservative and wouldn't buy them. But our
shoppers, who are much more sophisticated about fashion, recognize that
these designs are so dramatic that they are actually timeless. Many of the
designer clothes bought in the Basement store are worn for ten or fifteen
years."

THE BEST TIME TO BUY

As we've mentioned earlier, the January sales can save you tons of
money. They offer fall and winter merchandise and luxury clothing items left
over from Christmas promotions at prices usually ranging from 50 to 80 percent less than the original retail prices. Watch the newspaper ads beginning
December 24, which often state: "Sales begin December 26."

If you can budget $100 to $500 for the January sales, you can usually
buy anywhere from $200 to $2,000 worth of clothing, based on original retail
prices. (July sales are good, too, but they're usually not as spectacular as the
January sales.)

NETWORKING

You usually hear and read about networking in terms of career development, with the "old girl" network helping women professionally. To us,

though, networking is our own private "jungle telegraph" of eight or ten women who phone each other with news of advertised or unadvertised sales. We may sound like *yentas* (village gossips) to outsiders, but we love passing around and receiving news of great buys and adore the conspiratorial feeling that we're outwitting the stores and other customers (who may, for all we know, be part of other, similar networks).

SALE DIARIES

Sale diaries are another great help in long-term planning. They're pretty informal and generally consist of noting somewhere (usually in the back of our wardrobe-inventory notebook, because we always take it shopping with us) which stores have sales, on what dates, what merchandise was on sale, and what the markdowns were. After a couple of years, a pattern usually takes shape. Thus, after two years, we can guess approximately when in January Gucci will hold its storewide clearance at its main store, and approximately when it will move its remaining merchandise to its clearance store, Gucci on Seven (2 East 54th Street, New York City). We can also estimate when Macy's will hold its wonderful designer shoe clearance (fantastic shoes for around $30 a pair), and will make sure to have time and money to explore our favorite sales.

Our sale diaries will also note which stores have disappointing sales, so that we can avoid them in the future, no matter how seductive their ads sound. Any one sale can be a flub, so our rule of thumb is: three strikes, and it's out. And the store stays on our "hit list" until we hear good news about it from two or three trusted friends.

BARGAINING

Although American stores are a far cry from Middle Eastern bazaars, it's still possible to bargain sometimes.

Don't be afraid to bargain if you can find a tiny, insignificant defect, or if you know how long the item has been in the store. This ploy works best in small stores because there is less paperwork and going-through-channels involved in pricing. But sometimes this strategy will work in department stores if you can talk to a buyer or senior salesperson and have the garment reticketed. We were able to get a printed silk blouse from Gucci, originally $250, marked down to $79, for only $69 because we pointed out that it was the only blouse of its kind without an attached scarf. Even though the blouse had never had a scarf, we persuaded the Gucci salespeople that it should be priced less than a similar blouse with a scarf.

With all the marvelous advantages of clearance-sale shopping, there are still a few traps for the unwary buyer:

DON'T GO BROKE ON BARGAINS

Bargains are great, but don't wind up, as a few of our friends have done, overspending ("But look at all the money I saved!" they wailed) and getting into hot water with department stores and credit-card companies.

Here are some surefire ways to avoid going broke on bargains:

Keep track of your expenses, and cut yourself off when you reach your limit.

Ask yourself: "Do I really need this? How much do I want it? How/when/where will I wear it?"

Follow the "Rule of Three": If you can't think of at least three items you already own that this new garment coordinates with, or three ways you can wear it, put it back on the rack.

Keep your wardrobe in balance. If you have 30 shirts and blouses and only 4 skirts, don't buy another shirt or blouse, regardless of how great a bargain it is, unless it's a forced replacement (damaged by the cleaner, eaten by your puppy, hopelessly finger painted by your preschooler, etc.)

Make your next two or three purchases skirts, in order to balance your wardrobe.

And happy hunting—bargain shopping should be fun!

10
The Posh Stores

Most good stores and designer boutiques are worth inspecting every now and then. Even though you may not be able to afford their merchandise unless it's on sale, you can usually get some good ideas for accessorizing the clothes you already have and combining them in different ways.

Which are the posh department and specialty stores and boutiques? Even if you had just arrived in a flying saucer, you could find out in just a day or two. All you'd need is to ask which is the best newspaper in any city and check the ads in the front section (especially the full-page display ads). Look over the ads in the front section of magazines like *Vogue* and *Bazaar*, where the stores featuring designer clothes are listed, and the editorial content of the magazines, which also lists the stores that carry specific designer clothes. An hour or two scanning newspaper or fashion magazines in any strange new city should tell you which are the best stores and boutiques.

Another method we've often used is simply asking airline stewardesses when we're enroute to somewhere we've never been before. Cabbies can also be useful, even though they're men. Hotel personnel can give you good information and advice, too.

Because it's so easy to locate the best stores in your city, we're not going to waste time or space telling you which ones they are. You don't need our help here, as you might in finding discount stores, factory outlets, antique-clothing stores, and thrift shops. Instead, let's just plunge right in and tell you how to get the most out of the best stores in your area.

Every season fashion magazines focus on established and new innovative designers, and every season the best stores and boutiques in every city feature the most interesting of those designs. When you visit these stores, you can see, in three dimensions, what the magazines are talking about. You can try on the most advanced new fashions, see whether they flatter you, and think about whether you can adapt them by putting together clothes and accessories you already own.

The posh stores are also the places to learn about quality. When you try on clothes, look at how they are constructed, how they fit, how they feel, how they drape and move with you. You can learn a great deal firsthand, through your own senses, just by spending a half hour or so trying on clothes in a good store. Many items and looks can be copied on a budget. Rather than spending hundreds of dollars for a pair of Susan Bennis/Warren Edwards shoes or boots, for example, you can shop around and try to find a cheaper pair with a similar look. When a certain fashion look becomes accepted, it will be exploited by many manufacturers (the fashion industry calls this practice "knocking off") so it's usually possible to find a spectacular leather moccasin for $250 and a similar, decent copy for $25. All it takes is your sharp eye and a little time to hunt around for the copies.

Since the posh stores excel in service and have wonderful fitting personnel and comfortable dressing rooms, buy your bras and girdles there. Most good brands aren't discounted anyway, except for sales and New York's Orchard Street. If you're going to be spending the same amount of money for bras and girdles no matter where you buy them, you might as well enjoy the most comfortable dressing rooms and the best, most experienced fitters in town.

We like to browse in the posh stores periodically to see what's selling and what isn't. What isn't selling is certain to be marked down pretty quickly; these stores can't afford to carry their inventory for months because so much new high-fashion expensive merchandise (and expensive for the stores to finance at high interest rates) is coming in every week. Part of the high-fashion point of view is that everything must always be new and fresh, up-to-the-minute. If merchandise doesn't move quickly, it will be marked down again and again until it's sold—most likely, to bargain hunters like us.

Markdowns at good stores and designer boutiques can be incredible, depending on the stores' merchandising policies, inventory, time of the year, the national or local economy, and sometimes even the buyers' moods. Patient or just-plain-lucky shoppers often come away with unusual, beautifully made, high-quality merchandise for much less money than poorer-quality clothes in large chain stores. It's often simply a matter of the shopper's timing and persistence in casing clearing racks.

We've seen Bonnie Cashin cashmere halters at Saks Fifth Avenue marked down over six or eight weeks from $115 to $9.90. Smart shoppers waited for the ultimate markdown, confident that most women would think of cashmere halters as a poor design: anyway cashmere *should* have some kind of sleeve, and halters *shouldn't* be made of such a warm fabric. Besides, most women wouldn't want to try on cashmere in July, no matter how air-conditioned the store was. The clever women who *did* buy those halters were more flexible and imaginative in their fashion thinking. They may have planned to wear the cashmere halters with suits for after-work dates and parties, for spring evenings, and on chilly summer nights, with a shawl. Those women are probably giggling now when they see Zoran's similar cashmere designs for $200 to $250, and read the latest fashion philosophy, which espouses lightweight "seasonless" dressing and mentions sleeveless cashmeres as a perfect example.

Fabulous markdowns aren't just a New York or East Coast phenomenon. At Frederick & Nelson, our favorite posh store in Seattle, we've seen markdowns from 50 percent all the way to 97 percent throughout the designer department. A short black velvet Yves St. Laurent evening dress was reduced from $770 to $199. Calvin Klein bronze silk evening separates were reduced from $270 to $80.90 and $110 to $32.90. Bill Blass's avocado leather slacks were reduced from $170 to $59.90. And—our best buy for last—an enormous Yves St. Laurent scarf was marked down from $65 to $2.90!

Frederick & Nelson is our favorite West Coast store not only for its designer bargains, but also for the best service we've experienced in the United States. Even though it was our first visit and we were out-of-towners who might never shop at the store again, we were pampered outrageously and deliciously, plumped down on an elegant sofa and plied with coffee. After we had bought two or three things, the saleswomen asked us whether we could come back in a day or two. They told us that they'd be marking down their merchandise again and would have more bargains for us.

Finding great markdowns in good stores and boutiques is a game all its own—often with rules that you put together in your own mind as you shop more frequently and your experiences form patterns. You can't jump to conclusions based on one superb buy, but when the same sort of thing happens twice in a row in two different cities, you can draw some reasonable conclusions.

THE MORE MARKDOWNS, THE MERRIER

When we case clearance racks, we usually gravitate toward items with three or four markdowns, rather than just one. They're *always* either very, very bad—imperfect, shopworn, badly designed—or terrific buys that have been overlooked by shoppers because they were too high-styled, or an unusual color, or simply marked with a size that had no logical relation to its measurements.

Recently we bought Valentino's beautifully tailored navy cotton trousers, originally priced at $245, for $25. The markdowns alerted us that there was something odd about the pants, since the other clothes on the sale rack had only one or two markdowns, averaging 50 percent. Over what was probably a period of several months, the pants had been marked down like this: $245—$163—$123—$82—$49—$25. Even though the trousers were a size 6, the markdown was just too tempting, and we succumbed. Out came our trusty tape measure. Our eyes hadn't deceived us: it was one of the biggest 6s we'd ever seen! Of course, it fit and we bought it.

We assumed that the Valentino bargain was a pure fluke until something similar happened at Garfinkel's in Washington, D.C. about a month later. (We always investigate stores and boutiques when we travel.) This time it was another enormous size 6—a Perry Ellis skirt marked down five or six times from $58 to $6.

And then we realized that these tremendous bargains created by four or five markdowns (by this time, the store would almost be willing to give away the merchandise!) aren't all that unusual. Here's what we think happens:

Most women think of themselves as being one—or at most two—sizes, like a 6 to 8, or a 12 to 14. Because of this mind-set, they try on clothes in a very limited size range. The Valentino pants and Perry Ellis skirt ran very large, so women who normally wore size 4 to 6 or 6 to 8 and tried on the garments, which swam on them, put them back on the rack again. And again. And again. Women who wore sizes 10 and 12 never even thought of trying on a size 6—it couldn't possibly fit them! So these designer goodies just stayed on the rack for markdown after markdown, waiting for a sharp-eyed shopper who refused to be conned by the numbers game and believed her tape measure and not a size number on a price tag.

Men don't have these problems—or opportunities. Their clothing runs "true to size." Even allowing for the fact that French and Italian designs are cut closer to the body and British designs are generally a little fuller than American clothes, a man's suit size will usually vary by only one size number. If he wears a 40 Regular suit, he may occasionally need a 39 Regular or a 41 Regular, depending on the cut of the suit. If he wears a 16-36 shirt, that's the size that fits him at least 95 percent of the time. That's the major reason why men can buy clothes so quickly: they know *exactly* what size they wear, and it never changes unless they gain or lose weight.

But our situation is different: for women, sizes are virtually irrelevant. The masculine equivalent of a woman able to wear any size from a 6 to a 12 would be a man who could wear any size from a 38 Short to a 44 Long! Of course we understand that many women can wear a smaller size in a full skirt than a straight skirt, but the difference should be one size, not three. We'd love to see a more uniform sizing system; it would save women enormous chunks of shopping time.

Why the conspiracy on unstandardized sizes for women? Ah, the answers are simple! Designers know that women have been brainwashed into thinking that small (size) is beautiful, and that women who can crow, "Look, this designer 8 fits me!" will be more likely to buy one—or maybe even two or three, regardless of price—than if the same garment were marked 12 or 14. That's one reason why designer sizes run larger than cheaper garments. Another reason is that designer clothes are tailored better, are not cut skimpily to save that extra quarter yard of fabric that translates to 2,500 yards when 10,000 garments are cut.

There's another more subtle reason for designers', manufacturers', and stores' "agreement to disagree" on true sizing. They know that the more time a woman spends shopping in a store, the more clothes she'll wind up buying. If she can find her size in five minutes, she'll be out of the store in ten, having bought only one dress or blouse or skirt, or whatever. *But* if she has to spend twenty minutes just finding her size through trial and error, her eye will probably be caught by other garments as she thumbs through the racks, and she'll almost always buy more than one item.

That's another reason for the best clothing investment you'll ever make: your tape measure. Use it to quickly locate clothing in your size range. You'll waste less time and money, and you'll find super buys that other women overlook by their insistence on numbered sizes, rather than true measurements.

The posh stores can't be counted on for basics. You'll probably never find a navy blazer, gray skirt, black slacks or turtleneck, or white silk blouse you can afford because they'll be snapped up after one markdown, when they're still too expensive for most of us. (The blazer may be marked down from $400 or $500 to $200 or $250, but you may want to spend only $50 or $100.) Think of these stores for the caviar of your wardrobe, rather than its meat and potatoes. The suede blouse in the striking color that not everyone can wear, but that heightened your complexion or emphasizes your eyes. (Black women: you can wear many colors that would overwhelm us—the sale racks are a must for you.) Or the once-in-a-lifetime cocktail dress that you'll make your signature outfit for every party, as European women often do. Or the lizard purse that you'll use for years. These treasures can be found—and you can afford them.

11
Discount Stores

MANY BETTER clothes wind up in discount stores, often minus their status labels. Sometimes these garments are overruns: the manufacturer may have produced more items than he could sell through his usual retail channels. Sometimes they are the result of canceled retail orders. (These are the "manufacturers closeouts" you see advertised.) Sometimes the outfits are one-of-a-kind designer samples that are sold to discounters at the end of the season; and that can be the *selling* season, which is six months ahead of the time garments would ordinarily arrive in the stores.

Finding beautiful clothes at discount stores can be a hit-or-miss proposition. (Maybe that's why one large discount chain named itself Hit or Miss.) A shopper's chances of success generally depend on how often she visits the store, because both merchandise turnover and shopper turnover are much more rapid than in conventional retail stores. We've seen an entire rack of beautiful L'Eau Vive wool-blend pleated skirts disappear in just one hour at Alexander's—probably because they were only $9.99. And it wasn't even lunch hour! And our suburban friends around the country tell us that the most successful Loehmann's shoppers they know visit the stores every week or two. They don't buy every time they shop, but they do seem to increase their chances of snapping up beautiful clothes.

Loehmann's, with its fifty-odd stores around the country, deserves more

138

than just casual mention. Women seem either to love it or hate it, and either buy there almost exclusively or don't shop there at all because they've never found anything on four or five visits and have given up. The stores' advantages are the wide selection of discounted designer and middle-range clothing at the beginning of the season. Its disadvantages are the community dressing rooms, which women either don't mind or loathe, the lack of designer and manufacturer labels in most of the clothes, and the non-credit card, no-return policy. Loehmann's points out that the so-called disadvantages make it possible to offer designer clothing without upsetting the fashion industry and to discount its merchandise from 30 to 50 percent because it can minimize its overhead costs.

In addition to beautiful clothes at bargain prices, discount stores can also carry lots of poorly designed, badly made clothes at bargain prices which, in the long run, are really no bargain, but a waste of money. How can you tell the difference? By now, that's not a difficult task for you. Use what you've learned about fabric and tailoring to guide you. Simply looking at the fabric label is often enough, and will help you pull the two $7 wool sweaters from a table piled high with synthetics, just as it did for us. Remember to look carefully at how the fabric is matched at seams—especially if it's a stripe or plaid. And if it's done carelessly, don't even bother trying it on. Save your time and energy. Don't feel that you simply must buy whatever it is; outside of pantyhose to replace the pair you're wearing and just ripped, you don't need anything that desperately. There's always time to shop more selectively, and it's a must because discount-store merchandise is sometimes irregular or damaged.

There are all kinds of irregularities and damages. Some are inherent in the garment like a badly printed fabric, or a row of dropped stitches in a knit. Some irregularities are tailoring faults, like sleeve linings that are put in crookedly and twist the sleeve when the garment is tried on. Some damages happen in the store, like missing buttons, a broken zipper, a garment that a customer has torn or stained while trying it on, or sun-bleach damage to an outfit that's been exposed in a display window. Common sense will tell you whether the damage or irregularity is temporary and fixable. Replacing a broken zipper and lost buttons are easy jobs; fixing a crooked hem or lining isn't much harder. A soiled garment may be easy to wash; we recommend not taking chances on stained garments. Of course permanent problems, like the sun damage, should be avoided. If you decide to buy something that needs fixing, look over Chapter 6 for hints on alterations.

Let's focus now on the good clothes, the ones you will buy. If you love designer clothes, now there is a way to cope with stores having to remove their labels—or 90 percent of them.

Deciphering those tantalizing little shreds of labels that discount stores left in their designer clothes used to be a favorite game of smart shoppers. Some even used to paste pictures of designer labels in notebooks to match against the fragments. Fortunately, this exhausting little game is no longer necessary. Since 1976, the Federal Trade Commission has made designer identification code numbers available to the public in the *RN* (Registered Number) & *WPL* (Wool Products Labeling) *Directory*, which can be consulted in most reference libraries. (The code numbers are not mandatory, but most designers do use them.) These numbers appear on the left side of the designer label or on the tag that lists the fiber content of the garment. You may wish to copy the code numbers of some of your favorite designers and carry them with you whenever you shop.

Here are the RN and WPL code numbers of some popular designers:

RN	03005	Christian Dior	RN	31586	Lady Van Heusen
RN	14677	The Right Honour-	RN	31691	Donnkenny
		able Company of	RN	32203	Oleg Cassini
		Silk Merchants	RN	32493	Donnkenny
RN	14962	Lilli Ann	RN	33293	Geoffrey Beene
RN	16345	Vanity Fair	RN	33667	Porterhouse by
RN	16578	Catalina			Regina Porter
RN	16580	Catalina	RN	33752	Judy Bond
RN	16879	Judy Bond	RN	34104	Huk-a-Poo
RN	16890	Leslie Fay	RN	34972	Jonathan Logan
RN	17470	Villager	RN	35161	Bobbie Brooks
RN	18220	Sue Brett	RN	35195	Campus Casuals of
RN	19061	Lois Anderson for			California
		Tannerway	RN	35234	Huk-a-Poo
RN	19362	Rose Marie Reid	RN	35685	Evan-Picone
RN	24903	Donnkenny	RN	36236	Judy Bond
RN	25027	Liz Roberts	RN	36486	Act I
RN	25819	Bobbie Brooks	RN	36789	Act I
RN	25986	Judy Bond	RN	37448	Club House Knits
RN	26505	Suzy Perette	RN	37539	Suzy Perette
RN	27658	Suzy Perette	RN	37966	Jantzen
RN	27889	Judy Bond	RN	38344	Bill Blass
RN	27891	Judy Bond	RN	38494	Ship 'n' Shore
RN	29563	Lilli Ann	RN	38518	Bobbie Brooks
RN	30219	Stanley Blacker	RN	38554	Bobbie Brooks
RN	30669	Anne Fogarty	RN	38916	College Town
RN	30881	Bobbie Brooks	RN	39308	Leo Narducci
RN	31242	Villager	RN	39375	Cole of California
RN	31562	Cole of California	RN	39378	Cole of California

RN	39805	Lilly Pulitzer		RN	51454	G. J. Forbes
RN	40013	Happy Legs		RN	51488	Bal Harbour
RN	40679	Harvé Benard		RN	51832	Henri Pierre
RN	40803	Anne Klein		RN	52002	Liz Claiborne
RN	41327	Calvin Klein		RN	52130	Gloria Vanderbilt
RN	41443	Campus Casuals		RN	52992	Jordache
RN	41534	Pushbottoms U.S.A.		RN	53511	Kenar
RN	41550	Stanley Blacker		RN	53649	Huk-a-Poo
RN	41564	Halston		RN	54042	Daniel Hechter
RN	41567	Campus Casuals		RN	54516	Sasson
RN	41569	Campus Casuals		RN	54680	Huk-a-Poo
RN	42424	College Town		RN	55461	Les Halles
RN	42642	Calvin Klein		RN	55462	Les Halles
RN	42711	Leslie Fay		RN	55639	Stanley Blacker
RN	42960	Beene Bazaar		RN	55862	St. Tropez
RN	42992	Clovis Ruffin		RN	56168	Ralph Lauren
RN	43232	Jonathan Logan				Originals
RN	43517	Eccobay		RN	57272	Perry Ellis
RN	43857	Leslie Fay		RN	57302	Halston
RN	44278	Marisa Christina				
RN	44290	Jonathan Logan		WPL	01689	Lady Manhattan
RN	44597	Donnkenny		WPL	02278	Sasson
RN	44738	Lady Manhattan		WPL	02324	College Town
RN	46561	L'aura		WPL	03574	Cole of California
RN	46608	Chris Allan		WPL	03600	Cole of California
RN	46616	Halston Originals		WPL	06168	Bill Haire for
RN	47302	Bobbie Brooks				Friedricks Sport
RN	47396	London Fog		WPL	06549	TU's
RN	47398	London Fog		WPL	06979	Jantzen
RN	47400	London Fog		WPL	07887	Campus Casuals
RN	47478	DDDominick		WPL	08216	College Town
RN	47714	Leslie Fay		WPL	08428	Donnybrook
RN	48392	Stephen Burrows		WPL	08682	Evan-Picone
RN	48648	Anne Fogarty		WPL	08694	Alice Stuart
RN	48781	Catalina		WPL	09352	Oleg Cassini
RN	49528	Willi Smith		WPL	09442	Jonathan Logan
RN	50032	Oscar de la Renta		WPL	09536	Campus Casuals of
RN	50521	Bon Jour Paris				California
RN	50553	Donnybrook		WPL	10561	Nardis of Dallas
RN	50660	Donnkenny		WPL	11388	Stanley Blacker
RN	50976	A&F Originals		WPL	11390	Stanley Blacker
RN	51098	Irka by Bern Conrad		WPL	11798	Leslie Fay
RN	51331	Act I				

Since discount stores are either feast or famine for shoppers, stretch your clothing dollars by buying in quantities, even if you have to charge your purchases. Our most fundamental shopping rule is:

ALWAYS BE "OPEN TO BUY"

Retailers use the term "open to buy" to indicate their willingness and ability to buy interesting and unusual merchandise at the right price. Like these retailers, if you can draw on additional purchasing power—through savings or credit cards—and are not afraid to buy in quantity when the circumstances are right, you can save substantial amounts of money. Here are two recent real-life examples—both from Alexander's, our favorite New York area store—all the more so now that they've opened a branch in the World Trade Center whose early-morning hours cater to all us working people.

Right after the Fourth of July, Alexander's offered some magnificent Daniel Caron cashmere separates at prices ranging from $9.99 to $29.99. We scooped up a navy camisole ($9.99), cream skirt ($9.99), two cream wrap-style dresses ($29.99) to use as bathrobes—one for our city apartment and one for our farm. Even if we didn't have both city and country wardrobes, we *still* would have bought two of them: one for now, and one for later—four or five years from now. We think that you should buy a duplicate for future use if you find something special at a bargain price. Otherwise, when it's replacement time, your treasure will be either unavailable or unaffordable! We also bought two long, simple straight skirts—one red, one black—that double as strapless evening dresses ($29.99), and closely resemble Halston's designs of several years ago. (In Chapter 17 we'll show you how to make a similar long dress that you can wear half a dozen ways.) Total outlay: around $140 before sales tax for six beautiful, classic garments.

Then, recently, we suddenly found ourselves drawn to the leather and suede department at Alexander's. (For all we know, we may have an ESP for clothing bargains!) Sure enough, there was a rack of designer sample tops, jackets, pants and skirts, about 80 percent of them in one size—a 10. Many of the separates could be matched up as suits, which is what we did with a butter-soft periwinkle blue suede jacket and skirt and a rougher corduroy-rib suede hiking jacket with a bellows back and skirt in loden green. This was the second or third day of the sale, which we stumbled onto. Imagine what might have been there the first day! If we could have put together more ensembles, we certainly would have—that's what we mean by "open to buy"— because these beautifully detailed pieces were only $69.99 each!

MORE ABOUT SAMPLES

Just above, we mentioned sample garments. Why are they so desirable? Samples are made individually and as perfectly as possible because they are destined for the designer's or manufacturer's showroom, where they are displayed for department store and specialty store buyers. Orders for thousands of these garments hang on what the buyers think of the samples: how well they are designed and made.

It's easy to identify samples because they wear sample tags, which discount stores will leave on—if the designer or manufacturer permits them to —because they are powerful selling tools. In effect, they say, "I'm unique, I'm made much better than other garments. They're just copies of me and haven't been given tender loving care all the way from design to final production." Sample tags are 2″ x 4″ tags—usually metal-rimmed—which list the garment's model number, wholesale price, the size and color range in which the garment will be produced, and often fabric swatches in those colors. The wholesale price is usually half the retail price, and discount stores are often able to sell the sample garments for much less than the wholesale price. If you find a sample that looks well on you, grab it. It's a real bargain.

BE "OPEN TO BUY" OTHER THINGS, TOO

When the price is right, be ready to buy anything you need or like in quantity. For example, thanks to Leonore Fleischer's weekly "Sales and Bargains" column in *New York* magazine, which we recommend as a prime source of super-sale information, we went to a sale held by interior designer Angelo Donghia's fabric warehouse. What caught our eye was the announcement that this was the company's first such sale, and that all the fabrics were natural—cotton, linen, silk, and wool. (By now you must have caught on to our anti-synthetic bias.) The prices were so low that we staggered home with twenty five cotton remnants ranging from 27″ x 35″ and 54″ x 18″ up to 54″ x 95″—all for only $15!

Although it may not be apparent, we did shop selectively, even at these bargain prices. After all, a bargain isn't a bargain if you can't use it. What did we do with all this fabric? As we chose each piece, we had at least a vague idea of what we would do with it. Four small sample cuts—already machine-finished—made perfect placemats. We didn't have to touch them at all! One of the largest pieces—also already hemmed—became a tablecloth for our favorite host, whose dining room echoed the colors of the fabric. Some pieces were tagged to be made up as skirts, dresses, or suits, and some, we must confess, were simply bought to be put away until we could think of what to do with them because we knew we'd never be able to find fabric like that again at anything near those prices. (Remember: we paid only about 60 cents a yard for 54″ designer cotton fabric.)

When you get a chance at a sale like this one, think not only of yourself and of the current season, but of your future wardrobe and house needs, of gifts, and of your friends and relatives who sew.

Back to ready-made clothing, here are our discount-shopping recommendations:

ARIZONA

PHOENIX

The Back Door
2501 North Seventh Street

Bebe's Family Tree
2615 West Bethany Home Road

Geri's Sample Fashions
5824 North 16th Street

Loehmann's
3135 East Lincoln Drive

Maxine's Sample Dress Shop
Tower Plaza
3833-A East Thomas Road

Pic-A-Dilly Fashions
7 branches

CALIFORNIA

CHULA VISTA

Pic-A-Dilly
542 Broadway

DALY CITY

Loehmann's
75 Westlake Mall

Pic-A-Dilly
362 Gellert Boulevard

We Can Get It for You Wholesale
64 Westlake Court

EL CAJON

Pic-A-Dilly
863 Arnele Avenue

LARKSPUR

Pic-A-Dilly
2044 Redwood Highway

Reflections Ltd.
1115 Magnolia Avenue

LOS ANGELES

The Garment District
8822 West Sunset Boulevard

Harper's
331 East 12th Street

Judy Brown's
766 South Los Angeles Street

Loehmann's
6220 West Third Street

MONTEBELLO

Judy Brown's
2573 West Via Campo

OCEANSIDE

Pic-A-Dilly
1022 Mission Avenue

POWAY

Discount Clothing Warehouse
12332 Poway Road

RESEDA

Loehmann's
19389 Victory Boulevard

SAN ANSELMO

Pic-A-Dilly
914 Sir Francis Drake Boulevard

SAN FRANCISCO

Pic-A-Dilly
80 Post

SAN RAFAEL

Pic-A-Dilly
290 Northgate One

SOUTH SAN FRANCISCO

Outlet Store
221 South Maple Avenue

TORRANCE

Judy Brown's
20148 Hawthorne Boulevard

See also lists in Antique, Factory Outlet, Thrift, and Resale chapters

COLORADO

BOULDER

The Sampler
Highway 74

DENVER

Loehmann's
2400 East Hampden Avenue

Pic-A-Dilly
11 branches

The Sample Shop
2648 South Parker Road

Sample Simon
12970 West 20th Avenue

Sample Street
3095 Peoria
9186 West 44th Avenue

Sample Studio
10 South Havana

The Sampler
2982 Colorado

FLORIDA

CORAL GABLES

Empire of Hempstead
6917 Red Road

HALLANDALE

Syms
1950 SW 30th Avenue

MIAMI

Loehmann's
NE 187th Street and Biscayne
Boulevard

MIAMI BEACH

Empire of Hempstead
6987 Collins Avenue

NORTH MIAMI BEACH

Empire of Hempstead
1640 NE 164th Street

See also lists in Factory Outlet chapter.

GEORGIA

ATLANTA

Hit or Miss
3885 Peachtree Road NE

Loehmann's
3299 Buford Highway

Marshall's
4166 Buford Highway NE

COLLEGE PARK

Hit or Miss
4855-D Old National Highway

DECATUR

Hit or Miss
4570-D Memorial Drive

SMYRNA

Hit or Miss
2441 Cobb Parkway

Loehmann's
2460 Cobb Parkway

ILLINOIS

CHICAGO

Hit or Miss
    7 branches

Loehmann's
205 West Randolph

DOWNER'S GROVE

Loehmann's
1524 Butterfield Road

MORTON GROVE

Loehmann's
7118 Golf Road

INDIANA

INDIANAPOLIS

Hit or Miss
    Ayr-Way South Shopping Center
    3658 South East Street

    Honey Creek Shopping Center
    5416 West 38th

Nora Plaza
1300 East 86th

Washington Corner
9964 East Washington

KANSAS

BONNER SPRINGS

Clothes Closet of Samples
123 Oak

KENTUCKY

LOUISVILLE

The Sample Hut
3900 South Dupont Square

Sampling's Sample Apparel
1930 Bishop Lane

Sportswear Village
4155 Shelbyville Road

Wholesale Apparel
10504 Dixie Highway

LOUISIANA

NEW ORLEANS

The Classic Image
2089 Caton

Elle Est
1610 St. Charles Avenue

Josie's Clothing Outlet
934 Opelousas Avenue

MARYLAND

BALTIMORE

Hit or Miss
9 branches

Thirty Three 1/3
800 North Charles Street

BETHESDA

Fashion Tree
Wildwood Manor Center
10231 Old Georgetown Road

ELLICOTT CITY

The Clothes Connection
16 Normandy Shopping Center

FOREST HILL

C-Mart
1503-11 Rockspring Road

FORESTVILLE

Hit or Miss
Marlboro Pike and Forestville Road

GREENBELT

Fashion Factory
Beltway Plaza Mall
Greenbelt Road at Beltway Exit 28

LANGLEY PARK

Hit or Miss
7663 New Hampshire Avenue

LAUREL

Hit or Miss
Routes 197 and 198

The Store at Hub Plaza
Routes 197 and 198

OLNEY

Olney Village Mart
18220 Village Mart Drive

ROCKVILLE

Fashion Factory
785 Rockville Pike

Loehmann's
5230 Randolph Road

SILVER SPRINGS

Aspen Hill Shopping Center
13617 Connecticut Avenue

White Oak Shopping Center
12239-B New Hampshire Avenue

TOWSON

Loehmann's
1917 East Joppa Road

MASSACHUSETTS

ARLINGTON

Clothes Tree
1036 Massachusetts Avenue

BEVERLY

Marshall's
35 Enon Street

BOSTON

Ann Taylor Warehouse
872 Commonwealth Avenue
(sale second Tuesday to Friday
every month)

Filene's (basement)
426 Washington Street

Hit or Miss
6 branches

BROOKLINE

Bargains Unlimited
1328 Beacon Street
Coolidge Corner

BURLINGTON

Loehmann's
43 Middlesex Turnpike

CAMBRIDGE

Bargains Unlimited
601 Massachusetts Avenue
Central Square

FRAMINGHAM

Filene's
Route 30 & Framingham Mall

MATTAPAN SQUARE

Bargains Unlimited
Blue Hill Avenue

NATICK

Loehmann's
Route 9

NEW BEDFORD

Fashion Barn
605 Orchard Street

NORWELL

Your Advantage
Route 53

PEABODY

Marshall's
532 Lowell Street

QUINCY

Bargains Unlimited
1462 Hancock Street

SAUGUS

Bargains Unlimited
Saugus Plaza

Filene's
New England Shopping Center
Route 1

SWAMPSCOTT

Loehmann's
Vinnin Square Shopping Center

Marshall's
1005 Paradise Road

Your Advantage
Swampscott Mall at Vinnin Square

WELLESLEY

Your Advantage
200 Linden Street

MICHIGAN

DEARBORN HEIGHTS

Hit or Miss
5670 North Telegraph

FARMINGTON HILLS

Loehmann's
Orchard Lake Road and Fourteen
    Mile Road

MINNESOTA

BLOOMINGTON

Loehmann's
5141 West 98th Street

BROWSVILLE

Fashion SurPlus
Valley Ridge
1923 West Brownsville Crosstown

EXCELSIOR

Colette's Sample Shop
404 Second Street

MINNEAPOLIS

Carole's Sample Hutch
2726 East 50th Street

Fashion SurPlus
    Clover Shopping Center
    708 West 98th Street
    Normandie Shopping Center
    5224 West 84th Street

Hit or Miss
    8912 Highway 7
    2928 West 66th Street

Pic-A-Dilly
5225 Excelsior Boulevard

The Sample Hut
    5017 Excelsior Boulevard
    7822 Portland Avenue
    6530 University Avenue NE

Sample Mart
5406 Florida Avenue North

The Sample Rack
4313 Upton Avenue South

Westwood Sample Shop
2312 Louisiana Avenue South

ST. PAUL

Recie's Sample Shop
    1702 Grand Avenue
    1975 Seneca Road

MISSOURI

KANSAS CITY

Bea's Sample Shops
7327 West 80th

ST. LOUIS

The Sampler
8236 Forsyth

Sampler Boutique
605 North Jefferson

NEBRASKA

OMAHA

Le-Clothes-Out
1010 Howard

The Sample Tree
    3028 North 90th
    2774 South 129th Avenue

NEW JERSEY (metropolitan NYC)

EAST BRUNSWICK

Loehmann's
233 Highway 18

ELIZABETH

Daffy Dan's
1126 Dickinson Street

FLORHAM PARK

Loehmann's
176 Columbia Turnpike

FORDS

Syms
Route 9S and King Georges Road

JERSEY CITY

Bargain Bazaar
656 Newark Avenue

PARAMUS

Alexander's
Route 4

Bolton-Forman
171A Route 4 West

Empire Sportswear of Hempstead
132 West Route 4

Europea Imports
153 Route 4

Loehmann's
154 West Route 4

Syms
330 Route 17N

SECAUCUS

Designers Discounts
1161 Paterson Plank Road

Peta Lewis Outlet
116 Seaview Drive

WAYNE

Brandwagon
Preakness Shopping Center
1136 Hamburg Turnpike

WEST CALDWELL

Marshall's
Bloomfield Avenue

NEW YORK

BAYSHORE

Loehmann's
316 West Main Street

BRONX

Alexander's
2501 Grand Councourse

Empire
765 Riverdale Avenue

Loehmann's
9 West Fordham Road

BROOKLYN

Aaron's
627 Fifth Avenue

Alexander's
Kings Plaza
Avenue U and Flatbush Avenue

Loehmann's
19 Duryea Place

Lupu's
1494 Coney Island Avenue

S & W
4217 13th Avenue

BUFFALO

Sample Inc.
    10 branches

CEDARHURST

A. Altman
530 Central Avenue

Bolton's
86 Cedarhurst Avenue

EASTCHESTER

S & W
421 White Plains Road (Route 22)

ELMSFORD

Syms
395 Tarrytown Road

FLUSHING

Alexander's
Roosevelt Avenue and Main Street

FOREST HILLS

Empire
72-44 Austin Street

GARDEN CITY

Alexander's
Roosevelt Field Shopping Center

GREAT NECK

Empire
152-A Middle Neck Road

HEMPSTEAD

Empire
269 Fulton Avenue

HEWLETT

Clothes-Out
1739 Peninsula Boulevard

Empire
1 Piermont Avenue

Loehmann's
1296 Broadway

HUNTINGTON

Empire
325 Main Street

Loehmann's
301 West Jericho Turnpike

LYNBROOK

Clothes-Out
42 Atlantic Avenue

NEW HYDE PARK

Loehmann's
1550 Union Turnpike

NEW ROCHELLE

Bolton's
714 North Avenue

French Connection
683 North Avenue

Remin's
665 North Avenue

NEW YORK CITY

Alexander's
    World Trade Center
    Liberty and Church Streets
    58th Street and Lexington
        Avenue

A. Altman
    182 Orchard Street
    204 Fifth Avenue
    1341 Second Avenue

Berent & Smith
94 Rivington Street

Bolton's
    43 East Eighth Street
    53 West 23rd Street
    222 East 57th Street
    2251 Broadway
    1180 Madison Avenue

Damages
169 East 61st Street

Designers Connection
102 Orchard Street

Emotional Outlet
    91 Seventh Avenue
    250 East 51st Street
    435 East 86th Street

Empire
    469 Second Avenue
    1206 Second Avenue

European Liquidators
1404 Second Avenue

First Class
117 Orchard Street

Forecast
756 Lexington Avenue

French Connection
    1091 Lexington Avenue
    1397 Second Avenue
    1211 Madison Avenue

Grab Bag
2610 Broadway

J's Advance Apparel
491 Seventh Avenue

Jay Kay Retail Corp.
179 Orchard Street

Mern's
525 Madison Avenue

The New Store
289 Seventh Avenue

Peta Lewis
1120 Lexington Avenue

S & W
    165 West 26th Street
    283 Seventh Avenue
    291 Seventh Avenue

Syms
45 Park Place

Unlimited Pret a Porter
121 Orchard Street

REGO PARK

Alexander's
Queens Boulevard and 63rd Road

Loehmann's
60-06 99th Street

ROCHESTER

Sample Inc.
Long Ridge Mall

ROCKVILLE CENTER

Clothes-Out
324-A Sunrise Highway

ROSLYN HEIGHTS

Syms
250 South Service Road

VALLEY STREAM

Alexander's
500 West Sunrise Highway

WHITE PLAINS

Alexander's
60 South Broadway

Bailee's Limited
25 Tarrytown Road

Bolton's
Crossroads Shopping Center

Loehmann's
22 Tarrytown Road

WILLIAMSVILLE

Syms
7980 Transit Road

YONKERS

Alexander's
2500 Central Park Avenue

OHIO

CINCINNATI

Hit or Miss
    Casinelli Square
    8788 Colerain Avenue
    6212 Glenway Avenue
    704 Race

Loehmann's
Cincinnati Union Terminal

CLEVELAND

Clothing Outlet
31814 Vine

Fashion Warehouse
    442 Mayfield Road
    20195 Van Aken Boulevard

Hit or Miss
    6 branches

T J Maxx
6600 Biddulph Road

Sample House
5369 Warrensville Center

The Sample Shop
5836 Mayfield Road

Winner Designer Factory
1378 West Sixth Street

Winner Sportswear
1372 West Sixth Street

COLUMBUS

Hit or Miss
    932 South Hamilton
    3786 West Broad
    2025 West Henderson

T J Maxx
    5929 East Main
    2210 Morse Road

MAYFIELD HEIGHTS

Social Register
5110 Mayfield Road

SHAKER HEIGHTS

Melissa
28001 Chagrin Boulevard

PENNSYLVANIA

BALA-CYNWYD

Silk Threads
139 Montgomery Avenue

BETHEL PARK

Clothesline's Outlet
1787 North Highland Road

BRIDGEVILLE

The Clothes Bin
Great Southern Shopping Center

Hit or Miss
1025 Washington Park

DREXEL HILL

Loehmann's
1053 Pontiac Road

GIBSONIA

Sample Shack
5018 Route 18

MANAYUNK

Clothes & Things
4159 Main Street

MONROEVILLE

Hit or Miss
4051 William Penn Highway

MONGOMERYVILLE

Flemington Fashion Outlet
Route 309

NORTH WALES

Loehmann's
Routes 309 and 63

NORTHSIDE

The Clothes Bin
Allegheny Center

PHILADELPHIA

Brecher's Dress Shop
609 South Fourth Street

Brownie's
6722 Bustleton Avenue

Designers Discount Apparel
305 Market Street

Herb's Samples & Cancellations
1117 South Ninth

Hit or Miss
    1221 Chestnut
    9922 East Roosevelt Boulevard
    1129 Frankford Avenue

Montego Fashions Inc.
721-725 South Fourth Street

Shadow Clothing
39 South 40th

Silk Threads
8566 Bustleton Avenue

PITTSBURGH

The Clothes Bin
353 Fifth Avenue

Clothesouts
4764 Liberty Avenue

Designer Discount
638 Washington Road

Fashion Clothing Outlet
1627 Penn Avenue

*See also lists in Factory Outlet
    chapter*

TENNESSEE

GREENHILLS

Play It Again, Sam
2109 Abbott Martin Road

MEMPHIS

T J Maxx
4659 Knight-Arnold Road

Surplus City
    1026 Firestone Avenue
    2526 Highway 51S

NASHVILLE

Factory Connection
    Harding Mall
        3726 Old Hickory Boulevard

Hit or Miss
5346 Hickory Hollow Parkway

Nashville Apparel Distributor
157 Space Park South Drive

TEXAS

DALLAS

Direct Fashions Inc.
    8 branches

Loehmann's
11411 East NW Highway

Pic-A-Dilly
    5111 Greenville
    143 North Piano Road
    3265 West Camp Wisdon
    833 West Centerville

Suzanne's Discount Fashion Outlets
    11 branches

HOUSTON

The Buttonwood Tree
2609 Richmond

Loehmann's
SW Freeway and Fondren Road

Marshall's
    7051 SW Freeway
    plus 4 branches

Pic-A-Dilly
    9 branches

Simply Fashion
4056 Westheimer

Wearhouse 18
    174 FM 1960
    1911 Gessner
    9824 Harwin
    1005 NASA Road 1

POST OAK

Isabell Gerhart—Downstairs Store
Galleria

SAN ANTONIO

Loehmann's
Loop 410 and Summit Parkway

Margo's—La Mode
    6 branches

Sample Shop
    7415 Broadway
    904 Manor

Susie's Fashion Outlet
950 West Hildebrand

VIRGINIA

ALEXANDRIA

Hit or Miss
7666 Richmond Highway

Marshall's
Virginia Plaza Shopping Center
Routes 236 and 95

FAIRFAX

The Store at Hub Plaza
Pan-Am Shopping Center
Nutley Street and Fairfax

FALLS CHURCH

Loehmann's
7241 Arlington Boulevard

Syms
1000 East Broad Street

WASHINGTON

BURIEN

Pic-A-Dilly
205 SW 152nd Street

MERCER ISLAND

Sample Shop
7836 SE 28th

SEATTLE

Kay's Sample Shop
Terminal Sales Building

Loehmann's
3620 128th Street SE

Pic-A-Dilly
1005 Holman Road NW

Sample Fashions
122 15th East
612 Queen Anne North

See also list in Factory Outlet
chapter

WASHINGTON, DISTRICT OF COLUMBIA

Philipsborn Retail Outlet
1201 F Street NW

See also MARYLAND and
VIRGINIA

WISCONSIN

MILWAUKEE

Hit or Miss
8175 West Brown Deer Road

Loehmann's
10328 West Silver Spring Drive

WAUKESHA

Garment Gallery by Harriette
732 Clinton

12
Factory Outlets

SOONER OR LATER, many smart shoppers discover factory outlets and manufacturers' outlets, which are located away from the factory, but handle the same merchandise. Factory and manufacturers' outlets (we'll lump them together as "factory outlets" from now on) sell directly to the public at lower prices than retail because there are no delivery costs or retail frills. (Sometimes there aren't even dressing rooms.) Merchandise usually consists of overruns, canceled or returned orders, irregulars, samples, discontinued designs, and incomplete size ranges.

Factory outlets are one of the best ways to stretch your clothing dollar. Savings of 50 percent are common (this is our criterion for inclusion in the book), and savings of 75 percent and more are not unusual. By shopping at factory outlets, it's still possible to get three or four beautiful pieces for $100, rather than just one.

In addition to saving money, factory outlets have other advantages. Often you'll be able to find clothing after the "official season" in department stores has ended. And when you do, the clothing will be much fresher looking; it won't have been handled and tried on by hundreds of women. Often, too, you'll be able to find clothing before it comes to the stores in your area. Women who enjoy vacationing off season appreciate the convenience and freedom of choice of being able to buy bathing suits and lightweight sportswear in October or November, when they're unavailable in department stores, which begin to stock cruisewear in late December and January.

Many women who like wearing one-of-a-kinds love factory outlets because they can buy sample garments or limited-run designs in unusual colors.

Because most factory outlets are "no-frills" setups (remember, you always wind up paying for those little extras), you must shop very carefully. Many factory outlets have a no-return, no-exchange policy—even for Christmas presents. The no-exchange policy may seem harsh, but there's a good reason for it. Most factory outlets are simply not set up to reticket merchandise. Of course, there are exceptions. *If* you become a regular customer and get to know the salespeople, and *if* you need a size or color exchange of the same model once in a long while, they'll probably accommodate you. But don't expect it, and don't abuse the privilege.

Many factory outlets are cash only, or local checks with two or three pieces of identification. Plan on taking enough money and stash it away carefully. Pickpockets frequent factory outlets, too.

There are many little tricks you can learn to become a more efficient factory-outlet shopper. Most of them are also useful for other kinds of clothes shopping.

Always carry a tape measure. This is the biggest clothes-shopping time-saver we've ever found. Measuring the bust, waist, and hips of a garment before you take it into the dressing room (if there is one) saves not only time, but general wear and tear, and your disposition.

Carrying a tape measure can also help you *find* clothes as well as reject them. Twice in one month we found size 6 skirts that fit us perfectly, so it can't have been a freak occurrence. (We think of ourselves as a size 10 who can sometimes squeeze into an 8.) We would never have tried them on if we hadn't measured the waistband first and been delighted to see how big size 6 had become.

Become a "regular" if you like the merchandise. In the long run, popping in once or twice a month will save you lots of time and money. Just knowing the store's layout can help you find things quickly. And becoming a regular customer will usually get you better service and the one-of-a-kind buy, such as the sample that just came in that they haven't yet put out on the racks. Of course, you'll be put on their mailing list for private sales. And you'll also be able to find out whether any unadvertised sales or markdowns are coming up soon.

You'll also save time and money by learning the outlet's identification system and criteria for first-quality and irregular merchandise. And, if you become a regular customer, you'll be able to find out exactly how irregular an irregular really is, why merchandise was reduced, and other very useful information.

Always head first for the sale tables and racks. This is where the best buys are. This is the source of our favorite "brags": the $5 silk sweater, the $10 cashmere sweater, and similar goodies.

Learn the outlet's receiving schedule. If factory outlets receive merchandise after 5 P.M. every day, the best time to shop is early the next morning. If they receive new shipments once or twice a week, the best time to visit them is just after their deliveries. Saturday morning is usually a good time because factories often clear out their excess stock on Friday afternoons and send it over to their outlet store.

If you're the friendly type, chat with other women you meet at outlets. You can exchange information about clothes shopping—and other kinds of shopping, too. You may even plug into an informal shopping network, and you may even make new friends. How can you lose?

Before we discuss specific factory outlets city-by-city, two areas in the Northeast deserve special mention. One is the five-mile area in Bergen County, New Jersey, surrounding the intersection of Routes 4 and 17. Within this area are over a hundred factory outlets, discount stores, and shopping malls. If you live anywhere near this wonderful area, it pays to shop here—especially as an alternative to New York City's 8 percent sales tax. We suggest going with at least one other person, the first time, so that one of you can take notes while the other drives. Just cruise around and jot down where the interesting outlet and discount stores are. Break for coffee, if you like, and then go back and check out the most promising candidates.

Even Bergen County palls when it's compared with Reading, Pennsylvania, a city whose principal product seems to be factory outlets. Reading is so well known as "Outlet City" (for furniture and other items, as well as clothing) that charter buses have come from as far as 200 miles away. (Don't go to Reading on Saturdays, if you can help it.) Reading has half a dozen outlet *complexes*; some of them even have picnic tables and benches where shoppers can refresh themselves. After all, shopping in Reading is an all-day affair. Some of the major Reading outlet complexes are:

The Big Mill	*The Reading Outlet Center*
Eighth and Oley	*801 North Ninth Street*
The Great Factory Store	*VF Outlet Complex*
Moss Street between Spring and Perry	*Hill Avenue and Park Road*
(200 manufacturers represented)	*Wyomissing (just west of Reading)*

And let's not forget New York's garment district on Seventh Avenue and Broadway, where many manufacturers will sell to the public on Saturday mornings. The New York factory outlet listings later in this chapter are for manufacturers who will sell to the public during the week, as well as on Saturdays. For the others, who sell to the public only sporadically and often clandestinely—as part of the "underground economy"—the best thing to do is to get to 40th Street and Broadway or Seventh Avenue early on Saturday mornings and follow crowds. (Here's where a shopping network is extremely useful.) Elevator operators will know who's open and who isn't.

Check the merchandise very carefully: it may be irregular, and you may not be able to try it on. Sales will probably be for cash only, with no returns allowed. These rules may sound tough, but that's the way the rag trade is. Seventh Avenue can offer you great buys and great rip-offs. The more you know about design, fabric, tailoring, and what looks best on you, the more likely you are to be a successful factory-outlet shopper.

(Note: Not every city has a wholesale fashion district. If your area has none, your best bets are discount stores and the posh stores' January and July sales.)

Let us know what happens—and good luck!

ARIZONA

MESA

Fashion Distributors Factory Outlet
330 South Gilbert Road

CALIFORNIA

CANOGA PARK

Millard of California
6829 Canoga Avenue

CULVER CITY

Millard of California
4031 Sepulveda Boulevard

LOS ANGELES

Apparel City
752 South Los Angeles Street

Cachet International
860 South Los Angeles Street

The Clothing Connection
860 South Los Angeles Street

Designer Room
860 South Los Angeles Street

The Fantastic Designer Room
860 South Los Angeles Street

Fashion Reflections
860 South Los Angeles Street

Gerson's
327 East Ninth Street

International Designer Outlet
860 South Los Angeles Street

Millard of California
909 South Broadway

Sassons of LA
852 South Los Angeles Street

SAN ANSELMO

Lusty Ladies
137 Tunstead Avenue

SAN DIEGO

Factory Outlet
3967 Fifth Avenue

SAN FRANCISCO

Factory Outlet Store (junior sizes)
    101 15th Street
    654 Sacramento

Factory Store
    501 Bryant
    1151 Mission
    20 Second Street

Gunne Sax Ltd. Outlet
524 Second Street

In addition, there are about 100 manufacturers and wholesalers at 821 Market Street in downtown San Francisco. Visit these manufacturers early Saturday morning. Many of them will sell to the public for cash.

SAN RAFAEL

Clothes Factory
417 Third

COLORADO

DENVER

Check the Denver Merchandise Mart Saturday mornings. More than 100 manufacturers and wholesalers are headquartered there.

FLORIDA

MIAMI

Carlton Fashions
519 NW 26th Street

Jonathan Logan Factory Outlet of Miami
1640 NE 205th Terrace

Lilly Pulitzer Outlet
2801 NW 35th Street

Lorraine Designers of Miami
2480 NW 20th Street

Again, the usual comments. Here it's the Miami Merchadise Mart, 777 NW 72nd Street, that's the heart of factory-outlet action. But, since the Miami garment industry is more fragmented and spread out geographically than other garment centers, check the Yellow Pages and visit the local manufacturers.

GEORGIA

ATLANTA

Both the Atlanta Apparel Mart and the Atlanta Merchandise Mart house at least 100 manufacturers and wholesalers. Some manufacturers and wholesalers will sell to the public. Many of them will sell directly to the public in the morning. Some won't. This attitude may vary from week to week, every season, depending on overstocks, cancelled orders, and their need for cash as interest rates swing—mostly up.

ILLINOIS

CHICAGO

The majority of Chicago manufacturers and wholesalers are located in one easy-to-reach building: The Apparel Center. There's a little overflow into the Merchandise Mart and 337 South Franklin, nearby. Among these three locations there are 100 to 150 companies. Visit these manufacturers early on Saturday mornings, when many of them sell to the public.

KENTUCKY

LOUISVILLE

Fashion World Outlet
2504 Plantside Drive

In addition, there are about 10 manufacturers and wholesalers in Louisville; all are located at 1941 Bishop Lane, 1951 Bishop Lane, and 1870 Production Drive.

NEWPORT

The Mill Outlet Shop
Fifth and Washington

MARYLAND

BELTSVILLE

The Wearhouse
10766 Tucker Street

MASSACHUSETTS

ALLSTON

The Warehouse
44 North Beacon Street

CAMBRIDGE

Paramount Coat Company Factory
    Outlet
143 Albany Street

FALL RIVER

Fashion Factory Store
Weaver and West Streets

Franconia Sportswear
641 Quarry Street

Linjay Manufacturing Corporation
1567 North Main Street

Marvel Factory Outlet
657 Quarry Street

Robyn Wholesale Outlet
1567 North Main Street

NATICK

Coat Store
Route 9—1199 Worcester Road

WALTHAM

Handbag Outlet
406 Moody Street

MINNESOTA

MINNEAPOLIS

Minneapolis has about 100 manufacturers and wholesalers; names like Butte Knit, Dalton, Fire Islander, Koret of California, Leslie Fay, Ship 'n' Shore, White Stag, Wrangler. Nearly all of them are at the Radisson Center; the rest are mostly at 447 Seventh Street. Visit these manufacturers early on Saturday. Many of them will sell to the public for cash.

MISSOURI

KANSAS CITY

Kansas City has a small group of some 30 or 40 manufacturers and wholesalers. All of them are located at 1775 Universal Avenue, 1775 North Universal Avenue, and 1775 Universal Drive. Go early Saturday morning and be prepared to pay cash.

NEW JERSEY (metropolitan NYC)

BURLINGTON

Burlington Coat and Apparel Factory
    Outlet
Route 130

EAST RUTHERFORD

Leather Suedes Outlet
330 Murray Hill Parkway

ENGLEWOOD

McMullen Shop Factory Outlet
40 Rockwood Place

FAIRFIELD

Bee Hive Outlet Store (knits)
461 Route 46 West

FLEMINGTON

Flemington Fashion Outlet
Route 31 and Church Street

JERSEY CITY

Fire Islander Factory Outlet
111 Port Jersey Boulevard

LINDEN

Arthur's Limited Edition
842 East St. George Avenue

LIVINGSTON

Fashion Tree
437 West Mt. Pleasant Avenue
    (Route 10)

MIDDLETOWN

Fashion Tree
1040 Route 35

MOONACHIE

Factory Outlet (silk separates)
175 Moonachie Avenue

NORTH BERGEN

Palisades Outlet Store
7601 River Road

PARAMUS

Burlington Coat and Apparel Factory
    Outlet
Route 17S

PINE BROOK

Burlington Coat and Apparel Factory
    Outlet
Route 46

RUTHERFORD

Anne Fogarty Factory Outlet
13 Union Avenue

RUTHERFORD

Sweater Outlet of Rutherford
Outlet Mall
Route 17S and Paterson Plank Road

SECAUCUS

Chesa International Outlet
117 Seaview Drive

Abe Schrader Factory Outlet
Hartz Way

Wilroy Factory Outlet
1111 Secaucus Road

NEW YORK

COPAGUE

Burlington Coat Factory Warehouse
1187 Sunrise Highway

JAMAICA

Factory Outlet (Jonathan Logan,
    Villager, etc.)
183-04 Hillside Avenue

LAKE GROVE

Burlington Coat Factory Warehouse
2900 Middle Country Road
Jericho Turnpike

NEW YORK CITY

Abe Geller
491 Seventh Avenue

Gucci on Seven
2 East 54th Street

Irving Katz
228 West 38th Street

Miss Cindee Modes
270 West 38th Street

Ms., Miss & Mrs.
462 Seventh Avenue

Pappagallo Shoe Outlet
59 Fourth Avenue

Paris Fashions
270 West 38th Street

Saint Laurie
84 Fifth Avenue

St. Michel Leather
396 Fifth Avenue

Stanrose Dress Company
491 Seventh Avenue

Trendsetter (shearling and leather,
    wool coats)
        160 West 34th Street
        512 Seventh Avenue

Zynn Fashions (coats and suits)
270 West 38th Street
    (by appointment only)

OHIO

BOSTON

Dalton Industries
665 Broadway

CANTON

Dalton Industries
402 Second SE

CINCINNATI

White Oak Factory Outlet
   5800 Cheviot Road
   11469 Princeton Road

CLEVELAND

Dalton Industries
6116 Broadway

Winner Designer Factory
1378 West Sixth Street

WILLOUGHBY

Dalton Industries
4545 Dalton

PENNSYLVANIA

BERWYN

Lady Phillips
10 Leopard Road

BRISTOL

Importers Outlet
201 Basin Street

MANAYUNK

Clothes & Things
4159 Main Street

MONROEVILLE

See Pittsburgh

MONTGOMERYVILLE

Lancaster Dress Company
Routes 309 & 202

NORTH EAST PHILADELPHIA

Village Factory Outlet Store
Rockwell and Hartel

PHILADELPHIA

Barringer's Factory Outlet
Roberts and King Streets

Lancaster Dress Company
IVB Building
17th and Market

Larry's
2310 Chestnut

London Mills
3799 Jasper Street

M&M Factory Store
707 West Grange Street

New York Warehouse Outlet
231 Market Street

Northeast Factory Outlet
10175 Northeast Avenue

Shelley Shoppe
6609 Caster Avenue

Village Factory Outlet Store
4929 North Broad Street

Z Outlet Store
4736 Frankford Avenue

PITTSBURGH

Pittsburgh isn't known as a garment-
   industry town, but 90 percent
   of its 30-odd manufacturers are
   located in the Greater Pittsburgh
   Merchandise Mart Building in
   Monroeville. It's worth a try
   early Saturday mornings. Many
   manufacturers will sell to the
   public on a cash-and-carry basis.

SARVER

Hi-Ho Designer Factory Outlet
Ekastown Road
   (closed Monday & Tuesday)

TENNESSEE

GOODLETTSVILLE

Handmacher Fashions Outlet
705 2 Mile Parkway

MURFREESBORO

Warnaco Outlet Store
Park Avenue

NASHVILLE

Handmacher Fashions Outlet
712 Church
Windland Shopping Center

7th Avenue Fashion Distributors
107 Space Park South Drive

In addition to these factory outlets,
check 106, 117, and 157 Space
Park South Drive and 1808 West
End Building for other manufacturers and wholesalers who
may sell to the public.

TEXAS

DALLAS

Dallas is a major women's-wear center, like New York, Los Angeles,
and Atlanta. Most manufacturers
are located in the Apparel Mart
or in the vicinity of 2300 Stem-
mons Freeway. Manufacturers
and wholesalers usually sell to
the public, provided they're not
swamped—especially if the economy's been bad and they're

strapped for cash. Their attitudes
may vary from week to week and
season to season—fashion is a
very dynamic and high-strung
industry.

SAN ANTONIO

Cookie's Factory Outlet
447 West Hildebrand

Susie's Fashion Outlet
950 West Hildebrand

WASHINGTON

BELLEVUE

Jeans Warehouse Direct Retail Outlet
229 Bellevue Way NE

NORTHGATE

Jeans Warehouse Direct Retail Outlet
534 NE Northgate Way

SEATTLE

Jeans Warehouse Direct Retail Outlet
3157 Elliott
Pier 70

Over 90 percent of Seattle's more
than 100 wholesalers and manufacturers are located at the Seattle
Trade Center, 2601 Elliott. Some
companies may list the Trade
Center address and some the
Elliott Street address, but it's all
one enormous bargain-packed
building. Have fun shopping
door-to-door Saturday mornings,
and then head over to Pioneer
Square or the Pike Street Market
for brunch.

13
Antique Clothing

W E LOVE antique clothing.

As designers, we see the sources of modern designers' collections: Yves Saint Laurent's tasseled jackets with passementerie trimming had their origins in nineteenth-century Turkish designs and Napoleon III's Second Empire. Ralph Lauren's romantic "white look" was inspired by Victorian fashion, and Mary McFadden's characteristic pleating was originated by Mariano Fortuny in the early 1900s.

As shoppers, we think: "Why not buy these original designer clothes instead of their modern designer versions? The fabrics are more unusual, and the garments are more beautifully made and finished. The overall workmanship is much better. And—they're cheaper!" It's still possible to buy an original Fortuny evening dress for less than half the price of a modern Mary McFadden. And the difference in price, fabric, and workmanship between Victorian summer blouses, dresses, and petticoats (to be converted easily into skirts) and their modern versions is even greater.

We love antique-clothing auctions for the element of surprise: we never know what's going to be put up for sale. There's the bargaining aspect, the strategy and gamesmanship in competing against other bidders, and finally, if we're successful, the delight of getting something unique, unavailable anywhere else.

166

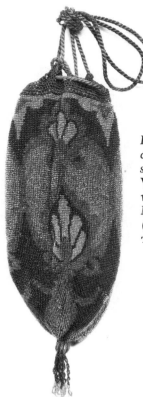

Exquisite antique beaded, mesh, or crocheted silk bags make inexpensive, charming evening accessories. Wrap the cord or chain around your wrist or attach the bag to your belt. Make it your personal trademark. (PHOTO COURTESY OF CHRISTIE'S EAST)

Sometimes, too, we get design ideas at auctions—not only from the clothes for sale, but also from what other people are wearing. We may meet colleagues at auctions and make contacts. Sometimes we make new friends.

WHAT CAN YOU GET AT AN AUCTION?

The kinds of clothes that are auctioned vary with the location and type of auction. Most country auctions will have some clothing—even Civil War and World War I uniforms—but clothing-only country auctions are very rare. Still, when they occur, they're usually worth attending because prices will be lower than in the antique-clothing stores whose owners pick up their stock at these auctions, and at city auctions, where the competition is greater.

Major auction houses like Christie's and Christie's East, Sotheby Parke Bernet, and Phillips, hold antique clothing auctions of "Nineteenth- and Twentieth-Century Costume," often combining European and American garments with Oriental robes and textiles. Often-collected nineteenth- and twentieth-century designers are Worth, Fortuny, Poiret, Callot Soeurs, and Vionnet for styles from 1880 to 1930 ("antique"), and Chanel, Cecil Beaton,

Take advantage of the growing Chinese fashion influence. These exquisite clothes are true art forms and can make sensational fashion statements for important evenings. (PHOTOS COURTESY OF CHRISTIE'S EAST)

Adrian, and lately Charles James for the 1920s through the 1950s ("vintage"). Most Victorian and Edwardian clothing—even the most elegant and beautifully made—is not known by designer. So far these top-quality auctions have been held only in London and in New York City; however, as women turn more to antique clothing for its originality and beautiful detail, auctions of this type will probably spread to other large cities.

Meanwhile, though, there are many vintage-clothing auctions all over the country. You may not find a mandarin's robes or Art Nouveau clothes from Paris, but you will find clothing from Victoriana to the 1930s, and sometimes even the 1950s. And the prices will be much lower than at the New York auction houses, where the quality is much higher, but because of competition from collectors and dealers and because of the prestige of the New York auctions, the prices are much, *much* higher.

In addition to the wonderful and unusual clothing at auctions, often you can find exquisite fabrics, antique shoes, laces and embroideries, buttons, purses, umbrellas and parasols, antique socks and stockings, modern copies of which are now being sold at astronomical prices (e.g., $30 to $40 for a pair of tights). For example, Christie's East recently offered these lots:

> six beaded bags, including one of silver and gold beads trimmed with beaded fringe, and one of silver mesh with chased frame
>
> a collection of accessories, including a violet silk parasol with braid trim; a fox shawl collar and cuffs; a brown lace bonnet trimmed with pink silk flowers and black velvet ties; and a wide-brimmed straw hat with a pink silk rose
>
> a collection of lingerie, comprising a pink silk teddy trimmed in cream lace, two ivory satin slips, and five pairs of lace-trimmed satin drawers
>
> a collection of Chinese embroidered cuffs and trimmings, including one of white satin embroidered in multicolored silks with flowers and buds; and another in royal blue satin embroidered in multicolored and gilt thread with prunus blossoms and butterflies

WHERE TO FIND AUCTIONS

Major auction houses like Christie's, Sotheby Parke Bernet, and Phillips advertise their auctions in *The Wall Street Journal*, *The New York Times*, and other daily newspapers, and in special-interest magazines like *Art News*, *The Collector*, and *Connoisseur*.

Local and country auctions advertise locally—often with posters and mimeographed notices as well as in regional newspapers. Usually these auction announcements appear on a specific day every week: check with your local newspaper to see which day is "Auction Day."

INSPECTING THE MERCHANDISE

Katie Kane, an antique-clothing dealer in New Hope, Pennsylvania, who specializes in Victoriana, suggests that antique-clothing buyers look for:

stains
rips and tears
previous alterations that might affect the value of the garment
signs that trimming has been removed

As a dealer, she is interested in what she can sell easily: authentic clothing in good condition that looks wearable—not too costumey.

Adventurous clothes lovers have much more freedom of choice and therefore can often find great deals at auctions. They can buy clothing that dealers cannot: clothing that can be redesigned or converted into a one-of-a-kind outfit. At Christie's East recently, we were the only bidders on this lot of clothing, estimated to sell for $60 to $80: a skirt of cream satin, appliquéd with pink chiffon rosettes with rhinestone centers and embroidered with shaped sequins and silver braid with looped garlands, *missing waistband* [italics in the catalog]; together with a pleated ivory satin cummerbund, an ivory satin slip with lace-trimmed bodice; and a cream taffeta petticoat with a chiffon ruffle at the hem (4 pieces).

We picked up the lot for $40 because no dealers wanted to bid on a skirt which was clearly the bottom part of a dress (remember the "*missing waistband*"). There's so much fabric in that Victorian skirt, which flowed into a train, that we're remaking it into a matching evening skirt and cape for summer formal wear. We already have several tops for it: silk blouses and cashmere halters in cream and black. The satin slip can be worn without alteration, and its lace bodice is perfect under sheer blouses; and the taffeta petticoat has been wrapped in tissue paper and stored in a trunk, awaiting inspiration and free time. The ivory satin cummerbund is frayed and may turn out to be unrepairable; even so, we still got three unique garments for $40 and look forward to creating a masterpiece for years of summer evenings.

Similarly, buyers who look at antique clothes as raw material, as well as completed garments, do not care whether they have been altered or whether trimming has been removed. Even rips and tears, which often bring clothing down to bargain-basement prices because they discourage dealers and collectors, may not matter if they won't show in a redesigned garment which is cut around them or which hides the damages within seam allowances or hems. Fabric that is brittle all over—to check it, carefully stretch fabric between your hands—is another story and should be avoided. Even the slightest pressure will shred it.

Stained clothing should be avoided, too, unless the stains can be hidden in redesigning the garments. Although many stains can be bleached out by repeated applications of diluted white vinegar or lemon juice and sunshine, many other stains are recalcitrant and seem to outlast the fabric itself. Maybe it's personal prejudice mixed with cowardice, but we'd sooner take a chance with a ripped or torn garment than a stained one.

BIDDING

Bidding at antique-clothing auctions is just like bidding at any other kind of antique auction. Here are the most important things to remember:

Individuals can generally afford to bid higher than dealers (but not collectors) because dealers are limited by profit margins and markups to approximately half of the price they will charge retail customers.

Do not get carried away and bid over the limit you have set for yourself. (This often happens when there are only two bidders left, and each one is determined to be the winner, to conquer all competition and emerge victorious with the trophy, even if it is most horrendously overpriced.)

If you're afraid you'll be caught up in the excitement of the auction and will bid over your limit, bid by mail and don't even attend the auction. (At that Christie's auction mentioned earlier, we put in bids on six different lots, but were the winning bidder on only one of them. If we had been there, we might have been seduced into bidding and winning all of them—and scrimping for months to pay for them.)

OTHER VINTAGE-CLOTHING SOURCES

In addition to auctions, there is a growing number of antique-clothing stores in major cities, which often advertise in "alternate life-style" newspapers and magazines. Even the staid *Wall Street Journal* recently featured an article on antique clothing.

Thrift shops and flea markets are iffy sources; the odds on finding anything at all can be low, and the odds on finding anything magnificent are much lower. What's worse, when they do have anything interesting, it may be priced as high as if it were in an antique-clothing shop.

One seldom-used source is little old ladies in your own neighborhood. They may be interested in disposing of some of their treasures—especially now, when their Social Security checks fall short of meeting their needs. Make people aware of what you're looking for, and that you're willing to pay cash.

And don't forget your older relatives: grandparents, great-aunts, in-laws, etc.

Here are some antique-clothing sources:

ARIZONA

PHOENIX

Sunset Boulevard
1003 East Camelback Road

TEMPE

Buffalo Exchange Ltd.
11 East Fifth Street

Dynabelle's Nostalgic Clothing
806 South Ash Avenue

Some Other Time
616 South Myrtle Avenue

CALIFORNIA

BERKELEY

Aardvark's Odd Ark
2552 Telegraph Avenue

HERMOSA BEACH

Aardvark's Odd Ark
810 Hermosa Boulevard

HOLLYWOOD

Aardvark's Odd Ark
7579 Melrose Avenue

LARKSPUR

Shadows of Forgotten Ancestors
503 Magnolia Avenue

LOS ANGELES

Auntie Mame
1102 La Cienega Boulevard

Bazaar Artistic
1404 West Vernon Avenue

Crystal Palace
8435 Melrose Avenue

Deco Flash Too
8530 Santa Monica Boulevard

The Gaucherie Store
5476 Marathon

Grandma's Stash from the Past
5533 West Pico Boulevard

Mariano Fortuny's dateless fashions are as magnificent today as they were sixty years ago, when they were made. These striking art forms cost far less than the contemporary evening wear of today's high-fashion designers, and should increase in value, too. Why buy a Mary McFadden when you can have an original Fortuny—the innovator and wizard of crystal pleating—for half the price? (PHOTOS COURTESY OF CHRISTIE'S EAST)

Junk for Joy
7739 Santa Monica Boulevard

Matinee
8722 Santa Monica Boulevard

Repeat Performance
7261 Melrose Avenue

A Store Is Born
5654 West Third

OAKLAND

Bizarre Bazaar
5634 College Avenue

SAN FRANCISCO

Aardvark's Odd Ark
330 Clement

Hot Stuff
1128 Polk Street

Matinee
1124 Polk Street

Old Gold
2304 Market Street

Painted Lady
1838 Divisadero

Pauli's Fantasy Clothes
400 Broadway

Poor Taste Collectibles
1562 Grant Avenue

Second Hand Rose
3326 23rd Street

Sh-Boom
6 Brady

Third Hand Store
1839 Divisadero

SILVERLAKE

Aardvark's Odd Ark
3906 West Sunset Boulevard

VENICE

Aardvark's Odd Ark
1516 Pacific Avenue

COLORADO

BOULDER

Golden Oldies Fine Vintage Fashions
2027 Broadway

The Ritz
959 Walnut

DENVER

Bertha's Rudely Decadent
1388 South Broadway

Collector's Choice Antiques and
        Vintage Clothing
2920 East Colfax Avenue

Herbert's Nostalgia
701 West Hampden Avenue

Little Annie's Fancy
2711 East Third Avenue

Molly's Vintage Clothing
1904 East Colfax Avenue

Nostalgia Shop
2431 South University Boulevard

The Ritz
1415 Lorimer

Vintage 78
2460 South Broadway

EVERGREEN

Feminine Collectables
5071 Highway 73

GEORGIA

ATLANTA

Annie's Hall
  Atlanta Flea Market
    92 Linden Avenue NE

Puttin' on the Ritz
3099 Peachtree Road NE

Sweet Emaline Antique Clothing &
  Accessories
994 Virginia Avenue SE

ILLINOIS

CHICAGO

Chicago Recycle Shop
5308 North Clark Street

Dallas La Mode Retro
3740 North Broadway

Follies Antique Apparel & Accessories
6981 North Sheridan

La Belle Nouvelle
70 East Oak Street

Second Hand Rose
3142 North Kilburn Street

WINNETKA

The Shirt Off Her Back
378 Green Bay Road

KENTUCKY

LOUISVILLE

Oldies But Goodies
1523 Highland Avenue

LOUISIANA

NEW ORLEANS

Mathilda's Antique Clothing
1222 Decatur

Second Hand Rose
3110 Magazine

Yesterday's Nostalgia Clothing
701 Dauphine

MARYLAND

BALTIMORE

Belle's Antique & Apparel Shop
7399 Liberty Road

MASSACHUSETTS

BOSTON

Bluefingers
101 Charles Street

Forever Flamingo
285 Newbury Street

BROOKLINE

RGF Antiques
195 Harvard Street

CAMBRIDGE

Atalanta Antiques
1168 Massachusetts Avenue

Ralph Lauren was undoubtedly inspired by the beautiful lace and hand-embroidered lawn dresses and intricately detailed blouses of the Victorian era. The workmanship of these original antiques is incomparable. These garments tend to be cheaper than contemporary designer clothes, and offer better fabric, detailing, and quality workmanship. (PHOTOS COURTESY OF CHRISTIE'S EAST)

MICHIGAN

DEARBORN HEIGHTS
Wardrobe-Plus Antiques
25534 Ford Road

DETROIT
Fabulous 2nd Hands
1437 Randolph

GREEKTOWN
It's the Ritz
1036 Beaubien

MINNESOTA

MINNEAPOLIS
Lois's Attic
2710 Lyndale Avenue South

MISSOURI

ST. LOUIS
Alice's Antique Clothes &
*   Collectables*
26 Maryland Plaza

NEBRASKA

OMAHA
Second Chance
1212 Howard

NEW YORK

BROCKPORT
Hand-Me-Downs
37 Main Street

NEW YORK CITY
The Best of Everything
242 East 77th Street

Cheap Jack's Antique Clothing
151 First Avenue

Dusty Rose's Born Yesterday
245 East 77th Street

Early Halloween
180 Ninth Avenue

Ethel's Feathers
189 Eighth Avenue

Fonda's
168 Lexington Avenue

Good Old Days
351 Bleecker Street

Good Old Things
155 Lexington Avenue

Jean Hoffman
236 East 80th Street

Jezebel Antique Clothing
265 Columbus Avenue

Kasbah
85 Second Avenue

Harriet Love
412 West Broadway

Lydia
21 East 65th Street

Ellen O'Neill's Supply Shop
251 East 77th Street

One Woman
336 Columbus Avenue

Ruby Slippers
243 East 60th Street

Joy L. Safran
by appointment: 832-8219

Trouvé
1200 Lexington Avenue

Tuna's Antique Fur and Velvet
160 First Avenue

Victoria Falls
147 Spring Street

PITTSFORD

Royal Rags
7 Schoen Place

Second Hand Rose
7 Schoen Place

ROCHESTER

After Eden
655 Monroe Avenue

OHIO

CINCINNATI

Downtown
119 Calhoun Street

A Patchwork Orange
2617 Vine Street

Remains to Be Seen
323 Ludlow Avenue

Scentiments
2614 Vine Street

Second Hand Rose
8286 Winton Road

Wearable Heirlooms
3161 Linwood Avenue

CLEVELAND

belladonna
1834 Coventry

COLUMBUS

AAA Bonnie & Clyde Antiques
2361 North High Street

Grandma's Antiques
1139 North High Street

Just Like Grandma's
1139 North High Street

J. Maroney
1776 East Main Street

Unicorn Collectibles Inc.
2 Chittenden

PENNSYLVANIA

NEW HOPE

Katie Kane's Antique Clothing
31 Ferry Street

PHILADELPHIA

Blue Gardenia
Sixth and Lombard

Judy's Place
255 South 29th Street

Panache
701 South Third Street

Rosebud
331 South Street

Tyler's
706 South Fourth Street

PITTSBURGH

Club Anonymous
284 Morewood Avenue

The Vamp
234 Shady Avenue

Yesterday's News
538 Brownsville Road

These simple, striking original suits by Adrian look very modern, although they were made in the 1940s. They have design details and finishing work found only in $500 suits today. Create your own unique style—even at work—with these vintage collectibles. Suit dressing needn't be boring. (PHOTOS COURTESY OF CHRISTIE'S EAST)

TENNESSEE

NASHVILLE

Nashville Ragtime
1406 Antioch Pike

TEXAS

DALLAS

Cliché
2804 Greenville Avenue

Eclectricity Antique Clothes
2002 Greenville Avenue

Faded Rose Antique Clothes
2720 North Henderson

Lulu's
3408 Oak Lawn

HOUSTON

Antiques & Things
127 West Southmore

Encore Resale Shop
2308 Morse

Ere Nostalgic Clothing
1831 Richmond

Leapin Leena's
422 West 19th

Yesterday's Rose Nostalgic Clothing
452 West 19th

SAN ANTONIO

String of Pearls Vintage Clothing
Boutique
109 East Locust

WASHINGTON

SEATTLE

Dreamland
1406 NE 42nd

Empire Antiques & Dolls
6740 Empire Way South

Fritzi Ritz Vintage Clothing
85 Pike Street

The Gibson Girls
5621 University Way NE

Refinery
5628 University Way NE

Sky King's Haberdashery
85 Pike Street

The Spare Room
1565 East Olive Way

Spider Grandmother & Sons
5214 University Way NE

Vintage Clothing
6501 Roosevelt Way NE

WASHINGTON, D.C.

Classic Clothing Co. Inc.
1015 Wisconsin Avenue NW
3701 Benning Road NE

Deja Vu Antiques
1675 Wisconsin Avenue NW

Geraldine's Vintage Clothing &
Costume Shop
4105 Wisconsin Avenue NE

Jameson & Hawkins
1522 Connecticut Avenue NW

Off the Cuff
1977 Wisconsin Avenue NW

WISCONSIN

MILWAUKEE
Not So Far from Zanzibar
1922 East Park Place

Sweet Doomed Angel
2217 North Farwell

Whiz Bang
1301 East Brady

Whiz Bang Too
1348 East Brady

ADAPTATIONS/ALTERATIONS/REPAIRS

Katie Kane emphasizes the originality and charm of her Victorian clothing, so she doesn't adapt or alter her clothes. She does make small repairs which do not affect the investment value of her antique garments—the kind everyone does on modern clothing: replacing the lace on the hem of a skirt, reinforcing loose hooks, eyes, buttons, and restitching open seams.

Dyan Siegel, another Pennsylvania dealer, whose store, Oasis, features "modern antique" clothing of the 1930s to the 1950s, is freer about adapting and altering her clothes because they aren't considered to be antiques which possess investment value. Dyan makes the same alterations that most home sewers do, and which we discuss in the "Recycling" chapter. If she finds an enormous skirt in a wonderful fabric, she'll buy it and take it in at the waist, or even recut it. Dyan will often taper the legs on baggy "zoot suit" corduroy pants from the 1940s because it gives them a better line and they're more flattering on her customers.

As we mentioned earlier in this chapter, we look at antique clothes both as what they are now, and as what they might become. We are not purists; we just love beautiful clothes made out of beautiful old fabrics. We have no qualms about adapting or altering clothing if we feel that we've improved it. (After all, evening dresses no longer require six-foot trains.)

STORAGE

Antique clothes must be stored carefully. Ideally, they should be wrapped in acid-free tissue paper (obtainable at art-supply stores) and stored flat in pillowcases or cardboard boxes, or hung on padded hangers in fabric garment bags if the fabric is not likely to stretch.

Never use plastic bags for storage. Delicate fabrics will deteriorate if heat and humidity are allowed to build up. Air must be able to circulate through and around them.

Never store starched clothing. Starch makes fabrics—especially cottons

—brittle, and they will eventually crack. Just wash the garment before folding it and putting it away. Iron the outfit just before wearing it, and spray-starch it, if necessary, but then it must be washed again to remove the starch before it's put away.

Never use perfume near antique clothing. It will make the fabric brittle and will eventually stain it.

ODDS AND ENDS

Old curtains and tablecloths are often made of wonderful fabric—yards of it! They're a good buy, too, since most people prefer buying antique clothes already made.

Old necklaces can be taken apart. Appliqué the beads and stones on sweaters and skirts. The uglier (usually, more elaborate) the necklace is, the less expensive it usually is—and the more raw material it provides. Save unusual buttons and trimmings and re-use them.

ANTIQUE MAKE-OVERS: STEP BY STEP

Transforming antique clothing into beautiful modern clothes isn't difficult; in fact, we think it's easier than working with a modern Vogue design that has twenty- or thirty-odd pattern pieces. Here are two antique make-overs we did—step by step.

White Linen Pillowcase into Summer Skirt

Linen pillowcases are always delightful to work with. They drape well for a soft look, but will starch beautifully for a crisper, more tailored appearance. They can be turned into skirts with just an evening's work because they need no hemming and no side seams.

We bought this linen pillowcase because of the fine tucking detail near the hem. This is how you can make the skirt we did:

1. Open top seam and try on.
2. Calculate where you want the hemline to fall and how much extra fabric there is at the top. Mark it and cut it across, allowing ½″ for seams. (For us, there was 4″ extra fabric, so we made our cut 3½″ from the top.) This will be your waistband.

3. Open the left side seam approximately 8″ and put in a zipper or a series of snaps. (Designers prefer to use snaps, especially on light-weight fabric.)

4. Now you're ready to decide what kind of pleating you want in order to take in the waist, which measures approximately 40″. Here are two suggestions:

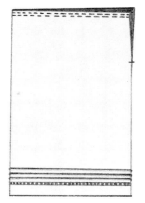

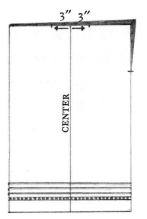

LEFT: *For lots of tiny unpressed pleats, run two lines of large basting stitches all around waist opening and gather to your waist measurements.*
BELOW: *For two soft inverted pleats—one front and one back—mark the center front and center back of the skirt at the waist. Calculate how much fabric you have to take in. For example, if your waist measures 28″ and the waist opening measures 40″, you're going to have to take in 12″—6″ in the front and 6″ in the back. Find the center of the front and mark it vertically with a pin. Then measure 3″ on each side of the pin and mark each point vertically with a pin. Now bring these side pins together so that they meet at the center pin, forming an inverted pleat. Tack or baste it in place. Repeat these steps to form the back pleat.*

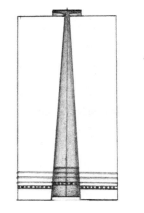

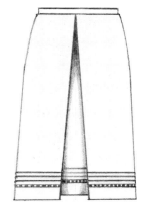

5. Now make the waistband to your measure, adding 1″ for overlap. Sew the side seams and top, making ½″ seams.

6. Sew the waistband to the skirt, starting at the back side of the zipper or snaps, so that the overlap will be in the front at the left side. Make ½″ seams. Sew hooks and eyes or snaps at the overlap.

TOTAL TIME: About 3 hours—allowing for trial and error—we're not very fast.

MATERIALS: Skirt zipper or snaps, hooks and eyes or snaps.

Cream Satin Evening Skirt and Train into Evening Skirt and Cape

This exquisitely ornate cream silk satin skirt, which may originally have been part of a ballgown, is festooned with sequins and chiffon roses with tiny rhinestone centers. Laurel wreaths decorate the hem and scalloped areas of the fabric, accented by a gathered ribbon bow. Small areas are flocked with magnificent cream silk motifs. To convert this into an evening skirt and cape, we used the following

MATERIALS

1 yd of 1″ cream grosgrain ribbon
6 hooks and eyes
2 yds of 3″ velvet ribbon   (We chose silvery gray, to accent the antique silver sequins and beads, but pink would have been equally attractive and would have highlighted the chiffon roses instead.)

First we removed the chiffon ruffle on the hem because we felt the garment would look more contemporary without the silk chiffon froufrou. (We saved the ruffle, of course, for future projects.) Because the scalloped hem was finished underneath the ruffle, we didn't have to worry about making a hem.

NOTE: Never pull or rip when you remove any trim or open seams of antique or vintage clothing. It's easy to harm the fabric underneath. Use sharp snipping scissors for this kind of detailed work, and make your cuts at least every ¼″. Pull out any leftover threads carefully with tweezers or very long fingernails.

Next we measured our waist and wrapped the fabric around it in order to decide where we wanted the detailed embroidery and beadwork to fall. We used the back panel as the center front of the skirt; because that panel was too narrow for the entire skirt, we measured 6″ from each seam and marked it with a pin. *Pin the fabric as often as necessary so that the final measurements and cutting will be exact and perfect.*
We allowed 1″ extra for seams. This pin point is the center back of our skirt.
We measured the hip area to make sure that there was enough ease across the hips and marked cutting lines and sewing lines for the center back.

SKIRT

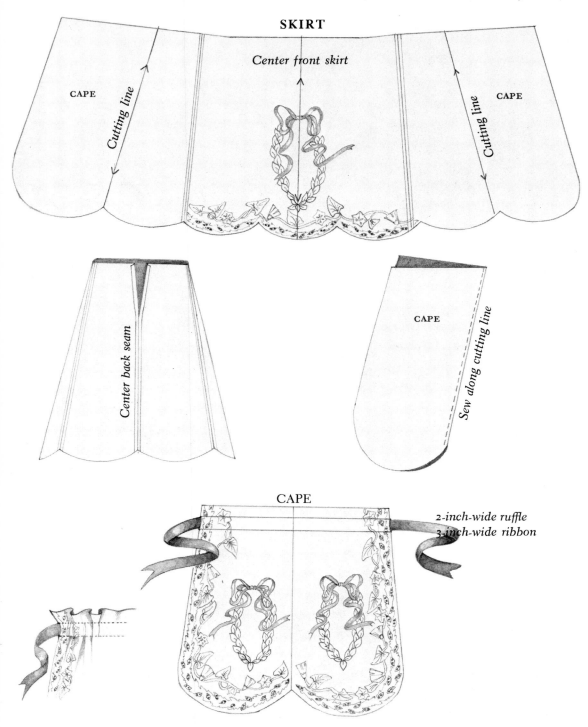

Center front skirt

CAPE

Cutting line

CAPE

Cutting line

Center back seam

CAPE

Sew along cutting line

CAPE

2-inch-wide ruffle
3-inch-wide ribbon

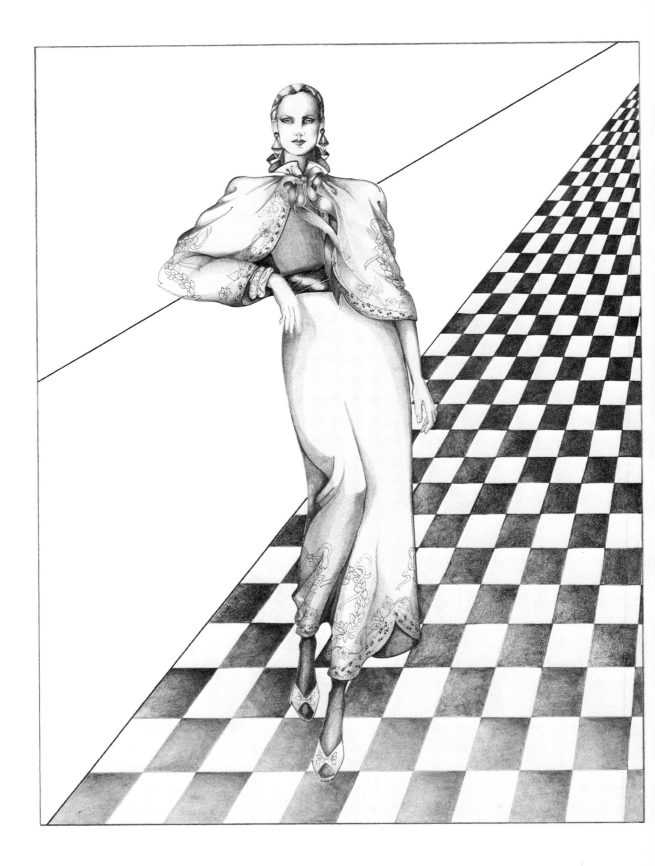

We tried it on several times, and when we were satisfied with the fit, we
made the two cuts for the skirt. The remaining fabric was used for
the matching evening cape.

We stitched the center back seam, but left it open 10″ from the waist
and then marked the finished length. Because of the ornate
scalloped hem, any adjustments in the length had to be made from
the waist. Then we marked the length of the skirt at the waist,
allowing for the grosgrain ribbon inside the waistband. We tacked
in the grosgrain ribbon and used hooks and eyes at the waist
opening. Because of the supple, fragile nature of the silk fabric, we
preferred hooks and eyes to a zipper, which would be too heavy and
would distort the fluid character of the skirt.

To make the cape, we seamed the remaining two side panels together up
the center back. The ruffled collar of the cape was made by turning
under ½″ of fabric at the top and pressing it. Then we folded up
5″ and hemmed carefully and—we hope—relatively invisibly. Then
we measured up approximately 3⅜″ from the hem and made a
casing for the 3″ velvet ribbon by stitching along the line and slid
the ribbon through the casing.

ALL THIS MAY SOUND COMPLICATED, *but all we actually did
was sew two seams—one on the skirt and one on the cape, finish a waistband, sew on some hooks and eyes, make a casing, and run some ribbon
through it. Even counting the measuring and fitting, it took only three
or four hours. And this is what it looked like when it was finished.*

14
Thrift and Resale Shops

THE FIRST TIME we saw a $15 cashmere coat in a thrift shop, we ignored it. The second time we saw one, we wondered a little about it, but passed it up. The third time we saw a cashmere coat in a thrift shop, we realized that the first two times weren't just freak occurrences, and we grabbed it. Can we help it if we're slow? Oh, yes, by now cashmere coats had gone up to $20. Inflation hits thrift shops, too.

We're thrift-shop junkies, and we're not alone. We feel very respectable now that *Money* magazine published an article on thrift and resale shops in its "Quality in America" issue. Thrift shops seem to attract a motley crew. There are, of course, the people who can't afford to shop anywhere else. But lately they're in the minority. Most of the people we've seen lately in thrift shops are at least middle-income and seem to regard thrift shops with the delight that archaeologists have in a fresh new dig.

Here let's digress briefly to resale shops. Resale shops usually sell designer clothes on consignment and split the proceeds with the former owners. They can be quite marvelous for pricey designer clothes—often just last season's, but now quite passé to their chic owners. One New York resale shop boasts a client who spends $35,000 a year on clothes, wears them once or twice, and then sells them. Prices are usually about half what the garments cost new, and most shops have seasonal sales.

Personally, we can't afford resale shops. We tend to make out much better in Filene's Basement and in Alexander's. Nevertheless, we do feel that they have a place in this book and recommend them to women who crave beautiful, half-price designer clothes.

Now back to thrift shops.

Thrift shops are great fun and a wonderful source of cocktail-party conversation. Take our emerald-green mohair skirt, which we wear semiannually, for Christmas parties and on Saint Patrick's Day.

"That's a beautiful skirt," someone is bound to say.

"Oh, do you like it?" we answer. "It cost a quarter." That usually kicks off an interesting conversation. It certainly livens up the party.

For us, and for many women we know, thrift shopping is entertainment. There's an element of surprise: you never know what you'll find. Many women build fascinating and unique wardrobes based on the principle: If it's interesting and costs less than $20 (or $10, or even $5), buy it. They've discovered that some of the most elegant outfits—or their components—can be found in thrift shops. That's why so many chic women and designers frequent them.

We use thrift shops as sources of inexpensive but elegant gloves (because we invariably lose at least one of them, sooner or later, and good gloves cost $30 and $40 a pair now); of interesting fabric (almost anything silk or cashmere—and if it's size 24½, so much the better, so that there's more fabric for us to use); old table linens and lace to cannibalize; millinery; and trimmings. Their quality and workmanship are superior to most of what is produced today. We've also found some unique extravaganzas we never could have afforded anywhere else—and might not have been able to find at any price:

Two alligator bags—one from the rue Faubourg St.-Honoré, the luxest shopping street in Paris
Chinchilla shrug from Bergdorf's—it cost us more to clean and reline it than to buy it
A beaded Norell evening dress

Generally, though, we don't recommend buying old furs. Used furs are no bargain unless they're incredibly cheap. As skins get old, they lose their suppleness, dry out, and begin to crack. And then they're useless, unless they can be recycled as coat or cape linings (we wouldn't bother because they might crack again, in other places), or throws for beds or pillows. Our rule of thumb: don't pay any more for a fur than you would not regret if it lasted only a season or two.

Some thrift shops are better than others. In general, Salvation Army,

Goodwill, and Amvets stores don't carry elegant merchandise. (The Goodwill on Berkeley Street in Boston is the exception because unsold merchandise from Filene's Basement winds up there.) The best thrift shops are run by chic charities. We would recommend—sight unseen (at least, until we had gone there two or three times and found nothing)—thrift shops sponsored by the local opera, ballet, and symphony orchestra, the Junior League, private schools, Ivy League colleges and alumni associations, famous hospitals, museums, Public Broadcasting System affiliates. Many suburban thrift shops have better merchandise than their big-city cousins. For some reason we can't explain, Hadassah and Women's ORT usually have marvelous merchandise; Catholic and Lutheran thrift shops don't.

Besides thrift shops, there are other, more transitory sources of fascinating finds: School, church, synagogue, charity, and block-association bazaars are happy hunting grounds for experienced thrift-shoppers. Great clothing buys for $1 to $5 are quite common. We like bazaars for offbeat costume jewelry, especially now that the retro look is in. For about $5 at our local church's Harvest Festival Bazaar, we picked up three identical rhinestone clips —perfect for dressing up anything black or velvet or both; an obviously, beautifully fake coral brooch; a pearl dog collar; a pearl rope; and a bagful of assorted trinkets. Old hats from the 1940s and 1950s would have been great buys, too.

Thrift-shop buying has its own strategy. Here are our four basic rules for happy thrift-shop buying:

> *Always take a tape measure.* We've told you why many times in earlier chapters.
> *Always inspect the merchandise carefully.* Somebody gave it away for some reason. A couple of tiny holes are probably acceptable if they are mendable. Massive stains and tears are not. (Thrift shops are supposed to reject unusable contributions, but they're often too shorthanded to do so.)
> *Wear a leotard and tights* (or something similar) *in case there are no dressing rooms and you have to try on clothes in public.*
> *Haggle.* It often works—especially if you're a regular, or if you're buying a number of items.

P.S. Donate your cast-offs to thrift shops, too. Make someone else happy, and make yourself happy with a tax deduction.

Here are our thrift-shop and resale-shop recommendations:

ARIZONA

PHOENIX

Arizona Humane Society Auxiliary
    Thrift Shop
1263 North Cave Creek Road

Bebe's Family Tree
2615 West Bethany Home Road

The Clearing House
714 East Maryland Avenue

The Clothes Tree
2619 West Bethany Home Road

Encore Boutique
9120 North Cave Creek Road

Fashions Anonymous
2719 East Indian School Road

Hadassah Thrift Shop
1641 East McDowell Road

Repeat Performance Boutique
6009 North 16th Street

SCOTTSDALE

The Echo
7120 Second Street

Scottsdale Girls' Club Thrift Shop
3523 North 70th Street

TEMPE

Buffalo Exchange Ltd.
11 East Fifth Street

Shady Lady Boutique
1843 North Scottsdale Road

CALIFORNIA

CANOGA PARK

National Council of Jewish Women
21616 Sherman Way

CARDIFF-BY-THE-SEA

Animal Care Center Thrift Shop
118 Aberdeen Drive

CHULA VISTA

Sabrina's 2nd Time Around
682 Broadway

DEL MAR

Chelsea Girl
2683 Via De La Valle

ENCINITAS

The Mad Leucadian
1430 N Highway 101

Mimosa
184 N Highway 101

Rags
568 First Street

ESCONDIDO

Recycled Rags
1111 East Washington Avenue

GLENDALE

Patina
511 South Glendale Avenue

INGLEWOOD

American Cancer Society Thrift Shop
201 North La Brea Avenue

LA MESA

Encore Fashion Resale Shop
8371 La Mesa Boulevard

LEMON GROVE

Adorable Affordable Resale
8257½ Broadway

LOS ANGELES

Animals Unlimited
7709 Santa Monica Boulevard

Boulevard Used Clothing
7860 Santa Monica Boulevard

Celebrities' Apparel
9045 Santa Monica Boulevard

Center Thrift Shop
8944 West Pico Boulevard

Council Thrift Shops
543 North Fairfax Avenue

Hollywood Used Clothing Store
7836 Santa Monica Boulevard

Los Angeles Free Clinic Thrift &
    Boutique Shop
133 South La Brea

National Council of Jewish Women
    429 North Fairfax Avenue
    12204 Venice Boulevard
    5217 West Adams Boulevard
    2652 West Pico Boulevard

ORT Value Center
8672 West Pico Boulevard

Vista Del Mar Thrift Shop
8560 West Pico Boulevard

White Memorial Medical Center
    Thrift Shop
1803 Brooklyn Avenue

Women's Auxiliary of The California
    Pediatric Center
1415 South Grand Avenue

MENLO PARK

Merry-Go-Round
713 Santa Cruz Avenue

NORTH HOLLYWOOD

National Council of Jewish Women
53318 Lankershim

POWAY

Humane Associates Inc.
13261 Poway Road

SAN DIEGO

American Diabetes Association
4096 30th

Apple Box Resale
    3009 University Avenue
    1134 Seventh Avenue

Children's Hospital & Health Center
    Thrift House
3590 Fifth Avenue

Fancy Lor-Ancy's
5277 El Cajon Boulevard

SAN FRANCISCO

Abbe's Nearly New Apparel
1420 Clement

Attic Shop
1040 Hyde Street

Bear-ly New (UCSF Hospital)
2512 Clement

Cathedral School Shop
1036 Hyde Street

The Encore
2335 Clement

Junior League Shop
2226 Fillmore Street

Once Removed—Mills College Thrift
    Shop
1000 Irving

Opportunity Shop—Women's
    American ORT
2628 Fillmore Street

Presbyterian Hospital Division of
    Pacific Medical Center
2018 Webster

Repeat Performance (San Francisco
    Symphony)
2223 Fillmore Street

SAN MATEO

Turnstyle
60 North B

SAN RAFAEL

Encore of Marin
11 Mary Street

SANTA MONICA

The Great Name
2315 Wilshire Boulevard

SOLANO BEACH

Another Year
415 N Highway 101

STUDIO CITY

Stars & Debs
12424 Ventura Boulevard

COLORADO

BOULDER

2nd Hand Blues
1212 13th Street

DENVER

Encore Shop
    2222 South Havana
    2120 South Holly

Janet Lee Shops
    1415 Havana
    2136 South Sheridan Boulevard
    4401 Tennyson
    7450 West 38th Avenue

Modern Millie's Dress Boutique
    15473 East Hampden Avenue
    6460 East Yale Avenue

Rags to Riches
2555 Sheridan Boulevard

Second Look Ltd.
2328 East Exposition Avenue

University Thrift Shop
600 Ogden

EVERGREEN

Potpourri
61 Main Street

FLORIDA

JACKSONVILLE

Hadassah Bazaar
24 West Duval Street

Hand Me Downs
4022 West University Boulevard

Junior League Thrift Shop
35 West Monroe Street

Liberty Street Flea Market
3802 Liberty Street

Nearly-New Shop
1417 Nira Street

New to You
7210 Atlantic Avenue

MIAMI

American Cancer Society
7210 SW 40th Street

Bargain Bazaar of Coconut Grove
3216 Grand Avenue

National Council of Jewish Women
Fashion Spree Outlet
7311 NE First Place

Papanicolaou Cancer Research
    Institute at Miami Budget Shop
182 NE 79th Street

Second Showing II Inc.
8504 SW 129th Terrace

The Second Time Around
4041 SW 96th Avenue

MIAMI BEACH

Entre-Nous Madame Ltd.
1154 Normandy Drive

Hebrew Academy Women's Thrift
    Shop
732 Sixth Street

National Council of Jewish Women
1800 Bay Road

NORTH MIAMI

Friends of Animals Thrift Shop &
    Boutique
724 NE 130th Street

Second Debut
712 NE 128th Street

GEORGIA

ATLANTA

Annie's Hall
    Atlanta Flea Market
    92 Linden Avenue NE

Encore
2140 Henderson Mill Road NE

Junior League Nearly New Shop
2343-B Peachtree Road NE

Second Hand Rose
    752 North Highland Avenue NE
    1653 McLendon Avenue NE

COLLEGE PARK

Lace Thrift Store
3935 Main Street

DECATUR

Chickibea
2136 North Decatur Place

ILLINOIS

CHICAGO

Entre Nous Designer Resale Shop
115 East Oak Street

Fashion Exchange Center
67 East Oak Street

Flashy Trash
2555 North Halsted

Hadassah House North Resale Shop
5039 North Sheridan

Lou Stein's on Diversey
646 West Diversey

Michael Reese Medical Center
    Thrift Shop
54 West Chicago

ORT Resale Shop
3326 North Lincoln

Ultimately Yours Resale Shoppe
2941 North Broadway

Y-Not Resale Shoppe
6116 North Lincoln

EVANSTON

Crowded Closet, Inc.
    824 Custer
    822 Dempster

Thrift House of the Junior League
    of Evanston
511 Main Street

HIGHLAND PARK

Hadassah House Resale Shop
1710 First Street

WILMETTE

Once More with Feeling
1167 Wilmette Street

INDIANA

INDIANAPOLIS

Almost New Shoppe
8974 East 10th

Council Thrift Shops
667 East 38th

Dorothy Kent's Nearly New Shop
2258 North Meridian

Jeanie's Corner Second Act Shop
3190 South Keystone

Like New Shop
2623 Shelby

New to You Fashion Shop
5216 North College Avenue

Next-to-New Shop
2019 East 46th

KENTUCKY

LOUISVILLE

Clotique
1827 Bardstown Road

The Cubby Hole
1420 Bardstown Road

Jane's Clothes Exchange
4129 Bardstown Road

Old Town Traders Consignment
* Shop*
1141 Bardstown Road

The Purple Plum
1612 Bardstown Road

LOUISIANA

NEW ORLEANS

Council Thrift Shop
2104 Magazine

Encore Dress Shop
7814 Maple

Hadassah Re-Sale Boutique
4900 Freret

Junior League Thrift Shop
4619 Freret

Just Stuff
3201 Burgundy

MARYLAND

BALTIMORE

Another Woman's Treasure
1047 Hillen Street

Second Act
4029 Frederick Avenue

BETHESDA

Montgomery County Thrift Shop
7125 Wisconsin Avenue

Think New
4933 Auburn Avenue

SILVER SPRINGS

Family Thrift Shop
8233 Fenton Street

Paris Flea Market of the Prevention
* of Blindness Society*
924 Wayne Avenue

MASSACHUSETTS

BELMONT

Open Door Thrift Shop
61 White Street

BOSTON

Beacon Hill Thrift Shop
15 Charles

Morgan Memorial Goodwill
*   Industries*
95 Berkeley
*   (Unsold merchandise from*
*   Filene's Basement winds up*
*   here)*

BRIGHTON

Hadassah Bargain Spot
1121 Commonwealth Avenue

BROOKLINE

Beth Israel Hospital Thrift Shop
25 Harvard

New England Deaconess Hospital
*   Thrift Shop*
185 Pilgrim Road

CAMBRIDGE

Christ Church Re-Threads
17 Farwell Place

Morgan Memorial Goodwill
    Industries
1116 Massachusetts Avenue

QUINCY

Clothesp'ORT
31A Cottage Avenue

Morgan Memorial Goodwill
    Industries
4 Parking Way

SOMERVILLE

Morgan Memorial Goodwill
    Industries
385 Summer Street

WALTHAM

Morgan Memorial Goodwill
    Industries
436 Moody Street

WEYMOUTH

Second Fashions
404 Bridge Street

MICHIGAN

BERKELEY

Bargain Boutique
2741 12 Mile Road

DEARBORN

Bargain Boutique
5704 Schaefer

DETROIT

Bargain Boutique
120 Parsons

Chameleon Resale Shop
17172 Livernois

Council Thrift Shops
    16531 Livernois
    3403 Puritan

FERNDALE

Clothesport
627 W 9 Mile Road

Hadassah Thrift Shop
224 W 9 Mile Road

MINNESOTA

HOPKINS

The Scarlet Trunk
915 Hopkins Center

MINNEAPOLIS

The Clothes Den
3953 Central Avenue NE

The Clothes Horse
1614 West Lake

Clothing Exchange
2705 East Lake

Council Thrift Shop
3010 Bloom Avenue

Fagin and Me
3500 Nicolette Avenue

Fandango
604 West 26th Street

One More Tyme
1839 East 38th Street

The Pink Closet
4024 East 46th Street

Osie's Closet
3539 West 44th Street

ST. PAUL

Elite Repeat
1336 Randolph Avenue

Next to New (Junior League)
1 East Seventh Street

WAYZATA

The Reclothery
18336-C Minnetonka Boulevard

MISSOURI

CLAYTON

The Loft Resale Boutique
7527A Forsyth

KANSAS CITY

Council Thrift Shop
4626 Troost

Junior League Thrift Shop
4509 Troost

Nearly New Shop
4137 Pennsylvania

Philharmonic Thrift Shop
6226 Troost

Things Unlimited Flea Market
817 Westport Road

ST. LOUIS

Act II
1 North Central Avenue

Clayton Resellit Shop
8409 Maryland

Encore Shop
9 Town & Country Mall

Hadassah's Clothes & Collectables
2527 Woodson Road

New Hope Foundation
227 Lemay Ferry Road
1901 North Florissant

The Not So Old Shoe
4578 Laclede

Rethreads
11605 Olive Street Road

Scholarshop
8719 Hoover

Second Time Around Shoppe
13145 New Halls Ferry Road

Wear Else Inc.
8109 Big Bend Boulevard

NEBRASKA

BELLEVUE

The Attic
2007½ Galvin Road South

OMAHA

Council Thrift Shop
623 South 24th

Hadassah Bargain Center
2913 Leavenworth

Jumble Shop of the Junior League
6104 Maple

Yours & My Closet
2221 North 90th

PAPILLON

The Clothes Hangar
107 North Washington

Joseph's Coat
122 North Washington

NEW YORK

BROCKPORT

The Castaways
80 Clinton

BUFFALO

Eleanor's Trading Post
2267 Delaware Avenue

Fripperie
425 Elmwood Avenue

Hadassah Thrift Shop
3047 Bailey Avenue

Junior League Thrift Shop
168 Allen

Lots of Clothes
746 Main Street

CHEEKTOWAGA

Act II
2405 Harlem Road

HILTON

Once Around Twice
22 Canning Street Square

KENMORE

Dee's Clothes Closet
2528 Elmwood Avenue

NEW YORK CITY

Animal Love Thrift Shop
1575 Third Avenue

The Center Thrift Shop (Post-graduate Center for Mental Health)
120 East 28th Street

East End Temple Thrift Shop
394 Second Avenue

Everybody's Thrift Shop
330 East 59th Street

Greenwich House Thrift Shop
273 Bleecker Street

Irvington House Thrift Shop
1534 Second Avenue

Memorial Hospital Thrift Shop
1410 Third Avenue

Repeat Performance Thrift Shop
1496 Third Avenue

Return Engagement
900 First Avenue

Second Story Ltd.
1400 Third Avenue

Stuyvesant Square Thrift Shop
1704 Second Avenue

Thrift House for Federation of Jewish Philanthropies
39 West 57th Street

Thrift Shop East (Federation of Jewish Philanthropies)
1430 Third Avenue

Trishop Thrift Shop
1642 Third Avenue

Zoe's Place Thrift Shop
181 West Fourth Street

PITTSFORD

Second Hand Place
7 Schoen Place

ROCHESTER

The Fashion Exchange
597 Stone Road

Hadassah Thrift Shop
470 Monroe Avenue

New-to-You Boutique
321 Driving Park

Spare Attire
332 Arnett Boulevard

The Wear House
920 Portland Avenue

WEBSTER

Second Time Around Fashion Boutique
175 Main Street West

WILLIAMSVILLE

Second Performance Shoppe
5947 Main Street

OHIO

CINCINNATI

Annie's Attic
8903 Reading Road

Bargain Center
1815 Vine Street

Cedar Chest
3515 Glenmore Avenue

Fashion Post Resale & Sample Shop
2681 Madison Road

Odds & Ends Thrift Shop
115 East 12th Street
1737 Vine Street

Recycled Threads
7722 Hamilton Avenue

Remains to Be Seen
323 Ludlow Avenue

Second Hand Rose
8286 Winton Road

Second Hand Rose East
1030 Delta Avenue

Women's American ORT
7530 Reading Road

CLEVELAND

Bargain Box—Women's American
ORT
3819 Lee Road
13018 Miles Avenue

Close Second
14939 St. Clair Avenue

Picadilly ORT
12202 Woodland Avenue

Second Story Exchange
12210 Woodland Avenue

Second Time Around
8162 Columbia

Showcase
11909 Buckeye

The Thrift Shops
11720 Buckeye

Westgate Resale
17118 Detroit

COLUMBUS

Children's Hospital Thrift Shop
1108 North High Street
1918 Parsons Street
260 South Fourth Street

Grove City Thrift Shop
4020 Broadway

Nearly New Shop
73 Maplewood Avenue

New Directions
2422 West Broad Street

PENNSYLVANIA

ARDMORE

Browse Around Thrift Shop
323 West Lancaster Avenue

Main Line Thrift Shop
27 East Lancaster Avenue

Nearly New Shop of the Hospital of
the University of Pennsylvania
26 East Athens Avenue

Penny-Wise Thrift Shop of
Jefferson Hospital
57 East Lancaster Avenue

Sort-of-New Shop (Women's
American ORT)
32 West Lancaster Avenue

BRYN MAWR

Junior League Thrift Shop
604 West Lancaster Avenue

Thrift Shop of the Bryn Mawr
Hospital
820 Glenbrook Road

FOX CHAPEL

The Hideout
1339 Freeport Road

MCMURRAY

The Hideout
South Washington Road

NARBERTH

Hamper Shop of the Lankenau
*   Hospital*
714 Montgomery Avenue

NORTH HILLS

North Hills Thrift Shop
7709 McKnight Road

PHILADELPHIA

B'nai B'rith Merry Go Round Shop
127 South 22nd Street

Community Service Society Thrift
*   Shop*
5621 Woodland Avenue

The Extra Hanger
30 Maplewood Avenue

Fight for Sight Thrift Shop
2027 Sansom

Frankford Hospital Thrift Shop
4912 Frankford Avenue

Hadassah's Another Chance
2006 Chestnut

Inglis House Thrift Shop
2600 Belmont Avenue

The Lady's Room
6258 Wissahickon Avenue

ORT Value Center
29 South 19th Street

Thrift Shop of the Federation of
*   Jewish Agencies*
1213 Walnut

The Wear After
6059 Castor Avenue

PITTSBURGH

Act II
800 South Aiken Avenue

The Clothes Horse
306 Beverly Road

The Hideout
Brentwood-Whitehall Shopping
*   Center*

Second Best
1325 Fifth Avenue

Windfalls
5105 Clairton Boulevard

WAYNE

Neighborhood League Shops
187 East Lancaster Avenue

TENNESSEE

MEMPHIS

Hadassah Thrift Store
944 South Cooper

Junior League Thrift Shop
1348 Poplar Avenue

White Elephant Thrift Shop
4491 Summer Avenue

NASHVILLE

Hadassah Thrift Shop
2821 West End Avenue

Second Hand Rose Boutique
4107 Hillsboro Road

Something Old Something New
*   Consignment Boutique*
4002-A Granny White Pike

Stuff
2213 Elliston Place

TEXAS

DALLAS

Baubles & Beads Resale Boutique
380 Promenade

Cliché
2804 Greenville Avenue

The Clothes Horse
116 East Main Street

Clotheshorse Anonymous Inc.
1413 Preston Forest Square

Fig Leaf Thrift
614 Hiett Avenue

Hodge-Podge
2603 Fairmount

My Sister's Closet
2522 Oak Lawn

Second Hand Rose
19711 Ferguson

Shady Lady
3422-A Greenville Avenue

The Too Small Shop
15 Richardson Terrace Village

Twice New Boutique
10149 Shoreview

HOUSTON

Act II Resale Store
304 West Main Street

Almeda Resale Loft
5708½ Almeda

Baubles & Beads Resale Boutiques
9039 Katy Freeway
820 WFM Road 1960
1955 West Gray
9715 Katy Freeway
971 NASA Road 1
2044 South Richey
9333 Stella Link

Between Us
3612 South Shepherd

Blue Bird Circle Shop
613 West Alabama

Houston Junior Forum Resale Shop
828 Heights

Second Debut Resale
10932-A Westheimer

This & That Re-Sale
4644 Beechnut
7503 Boone Road
14356 Memorial Drive

SAN ANTONIO

Act Two
1024 Donaldson

Barbara's Next to New Shoppe
112 NW Center Mall
5310A Jackwood

Cedar Tree
3739 Colony Drive

St. George's Episcopal Church
Thrift Shop
1917½ NW Military Highway

WASHINGTON

SEATTLE

Annie Mac
2213 NW Market

Children's Orthopedic Hospital &
Medical Center Thrift Shop
2026 Third Street

Classic Secondhand
219 N 85th

The Clothes Closet
4137 California SW

Cloud 9
6518 Roosevelt Way NE

The Gibson Girls
5621 University Way NE

Goodwill Shopping Center
Rainier S & S Dearborn

Mary's pop-ins
2123 Queen Anne N

The Silver Slipper Boutique
543-F NE Northgate Way

The Spare Room
1565 East Olive Way

The Wise Penny (Junior League of
    Seattle)
4744 University Way NE

ZOOLOOS
928 12th

WASHINGTON (District of Columbia)

Andre's Thrift Boutique
66 Farragut Place NW

Bargain Fair
2479 18th Street NW

Classic Clothing Company
1015 Wisconsin Avenue NW

Creative Recycling Thrift Shop
1214 H Street NE

Deborah's Place
1327 N Street NW

Encore of Washington
3715 Macomb Street NW

Secondhand Rose
1516 Wisconsin Avenue NW

Silhouettes of the Fashion Evolution
2700 Georgia Avenue NW

WISCONSIN

CEDARBURG

The Clothespin
W61 N517

MENOMONEE FALLS

Repeat Performance Boutique
    (Milwaukee Symphony)
N87 W16458 Appleton Avenue

MILWAUKEE

Act II Consignment Re-Sale Shoppe
4314 North Oakland Avenue

East Town Women's Resale Shop
104 East Mason

Elm Grove Resale & Sample Shoppe
13300 Watertown Plank Road

Hadassah Collectors Corner
3557 North Oakland Avenue

Little Orchid Annie
1327 East Brady

Lucille's Re-Sale Shop
3610 North Oakland Avenue

ORT Budget Shoppe
320 East Michigan

Thrift Shop—National Council of
    Jewish Women
3501 West Burleigh

Thriftique—National Council of
Jewish Women
3512 West Fond du Lac Avenue

THIENSVILLE

The Clothespin
222 North Main Street

15
Catalog Shopping

We ADMIT OUR BIAS: except for a very few places, we never shop by catalog. (After all, there's only one place to buy L. L. Bean moccasins!) Like most women, we prefer to shop in person. Even the best color reproduction in the most expensive catalogs can be misleading, if only because the paper is shiny.

There are other problems basic to the nature of catalog shopping. Many clothes—we think all clothes—should be tried on. And if they don't fit and make you look wonderful, they should be left in the store. They should not have to be repacked, dragged down to the post office, and returned with a request for a refund. The company you're dealing with may be honest, foursquare, and true blue—most of them are—but waiting for your package to arrive (often as long as eight weeks) and returning the merchandise if it doesn't fit or look becoming is still going to be a hassle. Unless you have four children under the age of five and can't get a sitter, or are a ranger in Yellowstone National Park, shop in person. If it means a shopping trip to the nearest big city once or twice a year, do it. Turn it into a mini-vacation, go to the museums and concerts, and shop in person. It's easier and faster, you're more likely to get exactly what you want, and you may find unexpected things as well (like an unadvertised sale) or run into an old friend.

Still, if you loathe shopping (we think it's exciting) or just can't get away, there are a few catalogs with unique merchandise that we do recommend. (When you order, if you're unsure of your size, send along a note with your measurements, and ask the company to send you the closest size. If you have a friend who orders from the company, try on some of her clothes to get an idea of how the company sizes its garments.)

For sheer wit and good humor, two T-shirt companies are superb. Outer Products (Box 88, Lafayette Hill, PA 19444) periodically publishes a catalog titled *The Journal of Academic T-Shirts*. Among its recent selections: Beethoven's Third Symphony (white on black); the periodic table of elements (navy on gold); and a diagrammed proof of the Pythagorean theorem (white on navy). For obvious reasons, our favorite is the proofreading T-shirt, full of misspellings and typographical errors, which features a marked-up poem titled "To Er Is Human, To Forgive Is Unusual," in blue on white. (The missing "r" in "Err" is elsewhere on the shirt.)

Historical Products (Box 220, Cambridge, MA 02238) features famous people, although there are a few novelties like the White Rabbit, Moby Dick, and Tyrannosaurus Rex. Feeling philosophical? Choose Schopenhauer, Nietzsche, or Bertrand Russell. Political? How about Malcolm X, Machiavelli, Mao Dze-dong, or Golda Meir? Mysterious? Wear Agatha Christie, Dashiell Hammett, Sherlock Holmes, Professor Moriarty, or Humphrey Bogart. The choice is overwhelming—especially since Historical Products offers not only regular and French-cut (tiny cap sleeves) T-shirts in a choice of colors, but also sweatshirts, nightshirts, totes and aprons (perfect choices: Carême and Escoffier). If you're still having trouble deciding, try the T-Shirt of the Month Club and let Historical Products choose for you.

All these T-shirts make marvelous conversation pieces. They're wonderful to wear when you've got the "new kid on the block" feeling at beach or ski resorts where everyone seems to know everyone else, and you want to stand out from the crowd and break the ice—but not blatantly.

For very unusual underthings and loungewear, Frederick's of Hollywood (6610 Hollywood Boulevard, Hollywood, CA 90028) probably has the widest selection. A year's subscription to their catalogs (11 issues) is $2.00.

Victoria's Secret (Box 31422, San Francisco, CA 94131) carries more elegant and expensive lingerie. The catalog costs $2.00.

For beautiful classic clothes, try the Talbot's catalog (164 North Street, Hingham, MA 02043). They've been selling the same tasteful, low-key sportswear since 1947, and they're a lifesaver when all the department stores are selling the kind of high-style Seventh Avenue fashions you just can't live with. But the clothes are expensive, and you may be able to find similar sportswear in other stores for much less money.

Similar in feel but more rugged is our favorite outdoor supplier, L. L. Bean, with the warmest, coziest gear and footwear to help make our Pennsylvania country winters bearable. (We may keep a roaring fire going from October through May, but someone has to bring in the wood!) At those times, we're especially grateful for Bean's flannel-lined pants, which we haven't seen anywhere else, except in kids' sizes. (L. L. Bean, Inc., Freeport, ME 04033).

And that's really about it for unique catalog shopping. For anything else, try to shop in person. It's guaranteed to be easier, and cheaper, too.

Part four

MAKE
IT
YOURSELF

16
Recycling

FAVORITE CLOTHES don't have to die. You can usually resuscitate them with a little imagination and know-how, as long as their fabric is generally in good shape. Stained and faded clothes can be dyed; worn collars can be replaced; moth holes can be camouflaged with lace and embroidery.

And not only old clothes can and should be recycled. What about those great pants that fit you perfectly across the seat, but are a bit too wide-legged to wear this year? Or that dress your mother gave you that is a beautiful color but has hideous lines? Grab your pins and measuring tape and get to work!

If you have never recycled your clothes before, start with old, worn garments, so that you're not afraid to experiment. Use clothes and trimmings you would otherwise throw away. That way, you won't cry if your first recycling efforts don't work; if they do, you now have something great to wear on weekends. As you gain experience, you'll also gain confidence. Soon you'll take recycling for granted and wonder how you ever managed before.

STAINED AND FADED CLOTHES

Dye them. There's no reason why an old red cotton shirt can't be transformed into a new navy shirt. Fabric dyes come in many colors, in both powder and liquid form. Cold-water dyes are not as readily available as hot-water dyes, but their colors are richer and don't run as much. Some garments can be dyed *only* with cold-water dyes, as we explain below.

Warning: Once you've dyed a garment, always wash it *separately*. Home-dyed clothes run like mad. But maybe you've always lusted after pink socks!

Before dyeing a garment, check its washing instructions. *A garment that must be washed in cold water must be dyed in cold water with cold-water dyes.* If you have always dry-cleaned your now-faded favorite, you have three choices: you can gamble on dyeing it in cold water, you can save it for at-home wear, as is, or you can use a technique other than dyeing to resurrect it.

Next check the fiber content. Most synthetics don't take dye well; blends of cotton or wool and synthetics vary from fabric to fabric. So if you're trying to dye a white skirt and blouse red, and one is cotton and the other is cotton/polyester, they will not come out the same shade.

Fabrics and yarns can be identified by a flame test: burning small swatches or a few threads of fiber. Using a candle or flame that does not produce its own strong odor, take a few threads of the fiber and move them slowly across the flame. Note the way the fiber reacts to the flame, how it smells when it burns, and the residue it leaves.

Cotton and *linen* are vegetable fibers. They smell like burning paper. They support a flame and leave a soft gray ash.

Wool and *silk* are animal fibers. They smell like singed hair. The fibers leave a crumbling dark ash.

Acetates and *triacetates* have a natural base, but are produced chemically. They smell vinegary and leave a hard dark bead.

Nylon, another man-made fiber, burns very quickly. Nylon blends are very flammable. Burning nylon smells like celery and leaves a hard tan bead.

Polyester smells sweet and perfumey when it is burned. It produces a hard tan bead similar to nylon, although it occasionally drips molten polymer. The best way to distinguish polyester from nylon is by smell.

Acrylic, another chemically created fiber, is distinguished easily by its strong chemical odor and hard black-bead residue.

Or, if the flame test is too much work, simply test-dye a small swatch of fabric. A strip from a seam allowance or part of the hem will do very nicely.

Third, remember that the original color of your garment will affect its final shade after dyeing, especially after a few washings. This is also true of stains: although dyeing a shirt that shared your spaghetti dinner will camouflage the stain, it won't cover it completely. If you really want to get a pure color—for example, if you want to dye a green shirt royal blue—you will have

FRENCH DESIGNER EMMANUELLE KHANH

. . . created these iris-inspired ensembles. For attention-getting results use embroidery and fabric pens to create your unique style.

to bleach it first. When you bleach a garment, you substantially weaken its fabric; but if you were going to throw it out, why not bleach it, dye it, and see what happens?

Now you're ready to dye. Use a plastic bucket or washtub—*not* your bathtub or sink. No matter how careful you are, you can wind up dyeing the porcelain, too, if its finish is worn or scratched. Wear beat-up clothes you won't mind ruining—the kind you'd wear to paint your apartment—and rubber gloves to protect your nails from stains.

Follow *closely* the dyeing instructions supplied by the manufacturer. If you are mixing two or more dyes for a special color, start with the lightest dye, then add the darker dyes a *little bit at a time* until you achieve the color you want. Old cotton underwear makes the best swatches for testing.

Don't rush the dye bath. Clothes look a few shades darker wet than dry, so judge the color accordingly.

After you've finished dyeing, fill the bucket or tub with cold water and add about one-half cup of white vinegar. Dip the freshly dyed garment in it three or four times before drying it. This final rinse sets the dye better than a plain cold-water rinse. Remember: always wash home-dyed clothes separately —in cold water—to protect the color and prevent it from spreading to other garments.

If you find dyeing in solid colors too limiting and want to be more creative, try painting with waterproof fabric pens or textile paints, both of which are available in most well-stocked art-supply and fabric stores. A little time and imagination are all that are needed to change dull, old, boring clothes into clothes that get compliments every time you wear them. Batiking is too complicated a process for this book, but if you know how to do it, try it on some of your old clothes for attention-getting results.

Or, if you're a better sewer or embroiderer than you are a painter, use ribbons, lace, sequins, paillettes, or appliqués. The choices are infinite.

If you can't find fabric pens, textile paints, and decorative trimmings in your area, ask these mail-order suppliers for their catalogs, and then get busy and crafty:

Herrschner's Inc.
Hoover Road
Stevens Point, WI 54481

Lee Wards
Elgin, IL 60120

Merribee Needlecraft Co.
2904 West Lancaster
Fort Worth, TX 76107

PAGE 217: *Change a simple shape into an art form using waterproof pens or textile paints.*

THE CAMISOLE

PAGE 218: *A key element of separates dressing. Decorate it by using embroidery or hand painting.*

PAGE 219: *If your clothes lack that individual touch the quickest way to achieve a difference is through color. Use these motifs as inspiration for embroideries or hand painting and get eye-catching results.*

WORN ELBOWS, SMALL HOLES, FRAYED COLLARS

Shirts and sweaters that betray how long they've been worn and loved can be salvaged in interesting and attractive ways. Sewing leather or suede patches on worn elbows is an old trick we've learned from our men. If you want to be able to throw your patched shirt or sweater in the washing machine, cotton chamois or heavy brushed denim makes handsome patches that wash well, too. Worn edges on collars and cuffs can be hidden—and a Chanel look added at the same time—with foldover braid.

Small holes, tears, and spots on the front of a shirt or sweater can be covered by embroidery, appliqués, and decorative ribbons or lace. Rescue a sweater that has runs around the neckline by sewing on appliqués or delicate leaves and flowers for a garlanded effect.

Two lacy handkerchiefs will make a beautiful old-fashioned yoke for the

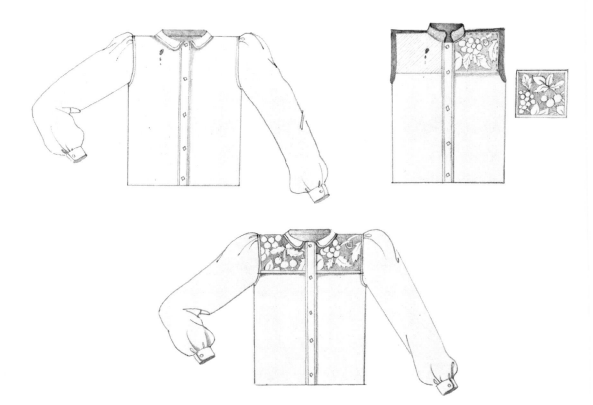

OLD-FASHIONED YOKE FROM TWO HANDKERCHIEFS

front of a silky blouse. *Carefully* open the sleeve and shoulder seams; if the holes left by the stitching are not clearly visible, mark the seam line and gathering with tailor's chalk. Lay the handkerchiefs over the front of the blouse, with the lower edge falling just above or below the fullest point of your bust. Baste each handkerchief to the shirt *inside* the seam allowance. Reclose the seams, then hem the right-hand handkerchief under the collar and under the placket of the right side of the blouse.

Remove the buttons on the left side of the blouse, under the left handkerchief, and mark their place with tailor's chalk. Hem the handkerchief to the front facing and under the collar of the blouse and re-attach the buttons.

PAGE 221: WORN ELBOWS, SMALL HOLES, FRAYED COLLARS

LEFT: *Recycle your stained blouse with appliqués; bind worn edges with ribbon.*
RIGHT: *Cover small holes with lace.*
BOTTOM LEFT: *Rescue a sweater with sequins and leaf appliqués.*
CENTER: *Use braid for the Chanel look.*
RIGHT: *Replace worn collars with lace.*

BLOUSE WITH NEW LACE SLEEVES AND JABOT

A stain or hole in your blouse sleeve doesn't mean that it's ready to be trashed. Remove the sleeve and use it as a pattern for cutting two new sleeves out of a coordinating lace fabric. Remember to add an extra ½″ for the seam allowance. Re-cut the cuff, too, to re-create the original sleeve in lace. Then sew the sleeves to the body of the blouse. There's nothing more sexy and appealing than a subtly revealing blouse like this one, with its new lace sleeves. If you like, add another touch of lace to the collar or add a coordinating jabot to pull this feminine look together in a flirty new blouse.

If you know how to embroider, you can save virtually any shirt or sweater with minor damages. We keep a graph-paper notebook with our favorite embroidery patterns. When a small hole, tear, stain, or other minor disaster occurs, out comes the notebook, and the shirt or sweater damage is quickly transformed into an ornament. The Dover Books line of needlework books is an excellent resource for all kinds of embroidery motifs, from various historical periods and cultures (see Bibliography).

But remember: if you appliqué or embroider your clothes without keeping the overall look of the garments in mind, they will look patched, not creative. This type of repair can't be done haphazardly.

A sweater or blouse with many small holes can be resurrected in several ways: with enough sequins, beads, or large paillettes to camouflage the holes; with embroidery that pulls off the same trick; or with lace in tiny rosettes or layered over the entire garment.

Following the basic directions to insert lace sleeves, earlier in this chapter, take the garment apart and use it as a pattern to cut another identical garment out of lace fabric. (If you are using this technique to rescue a sweater with ribbed collar and cuffs, you will wind up trimming the lace to the point where the ribbing starts, and tacking it in place.) Remember to add ½″ for seam allowance on all sides. If the lace has large motifs, center or place them carefully.

Then, basting first to keep the lace in place, with right sides together, sew all seams and make hems.

Torn or stained scarves are also recyclable. Turn them into colorful, casual necklaces. Stitch up any rips. Then fold the scarf into a long rectangle to cover the stains or repaired tears. Keeping the scarf pulled taut, knot it at 3″ intervals. Tack down the knots, being careful to conceal your stitches. Then tie the ends behind your neck, and your new necklace is ready.

STAINED SCARVES KNOT INTO COLORFUL NECKLACES

Frayed shirt collars? Simply open the seams where the collar is attached to the shirt and remove the collar. You can either leave the shirt collarless, cover it with a separate lace or crocheted collar, or attach gathered lace, eyelet, or ribbon. For a sportive look, cover a frayed collar with striped ribbon, then add matching epaulets. You may wish to add ribbon trim to the pockets, too.

Here's an easy change of silhouette. Add temporary padded shoulders that can be switched from garment to garment by tacking shoulder pads in a T-shirt and wearing it under sweaters, shirts, and blouses. If you like several different thicknesses of shoulder padding, you can use snaps to snap in whichever set of shoulder pads works best with each outfit.

Old flared, gathered, or baggy pants can be transformed, too. For "city shorts," one of the new looks of the 1980s, just shorten the pants to mid-knee and add a 1″ cuff. It shouldn't take more than an hour or two, and you can make the hems while you watch TV.

Knickers and bloomers, two popular new pants looks, can also be made from old slacks. Cut off the bottom of each leg approximately 2½″ below the knee. Use the cut-off pieces to make new cuffs anywhere from 1″ to 4″ wide. (Bloomers often have wider cuffs than knickers.) Add topstitching and buttons to the cuffs, if you like. Pin the cuffs to the shortened pant leg, easing the fabric into the cuff by gathering or tucking, and making sure to balance the fullness around the knee.

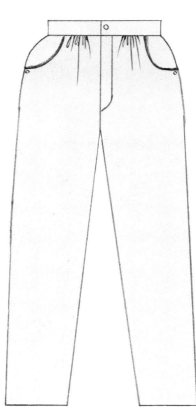

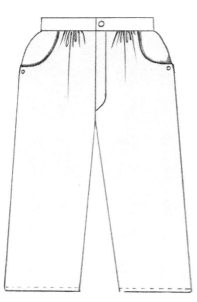

OLD SLACKS TRANSFORMED
INTO WONDERFUL KNICKERS

Old flared pants can also be transformed into wonderful skirts. This redesigning also enlarges the garment through the hips, so it's a great solution to the problem of what to do with beautiful pants that are now too tight. Try the pants on and mark the length you want your finished skirt hem to be. Cut the pants off approximately 3″ below that point to allow for hemming.

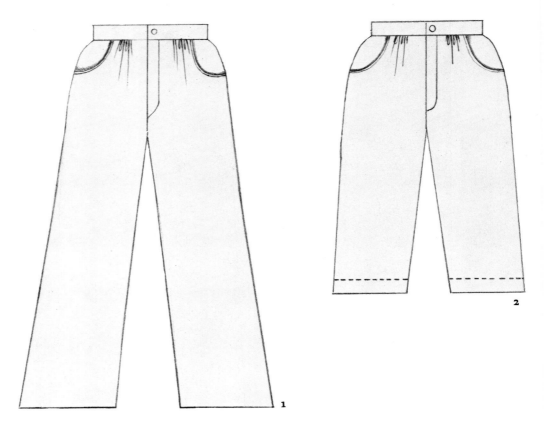

PAGES 226–229: FLARED PANTS TRANSFORMED INTO A SKIRT

With a seam ripper or manicure scissors, carefully open the entire inner leg seam so that there is no division between the pant legs. You will also have to open the crotch seat several inches in front and in back. Turn under the fabric until the new openings are clean and smooth, and pin in place. Adjust the edges of the openings, baste, and trim away the excess fabric in both the front and the back, allowing ⅝″ for seams.

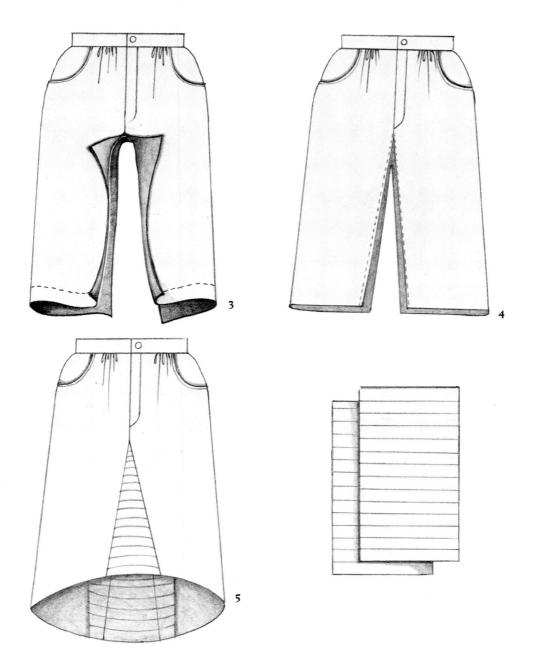

The fabric for the skirt insets should be similar in weight to the pants fabric. One yard of 36″ fabric is usually enough. Lay the skirt-to-be on a flat surface and measure the skirt opening at its widest point (the hem). Measure the length from the hem to the top of the insert. Add 2″ to the length and width measurements and cut two rectangles. Center the rectangles in the

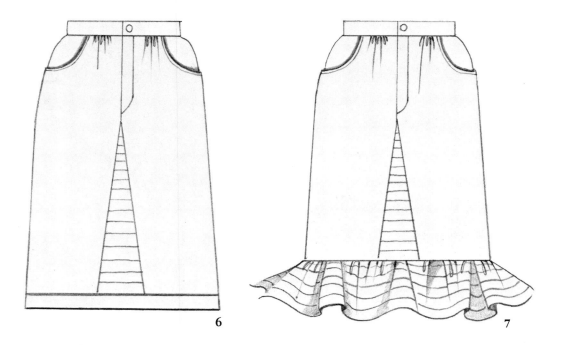

6   7

front and back openings and pin. Try on the skirt to make sure that the skirt falls nicely. Also check the length. Remember: wear shoes with the heel height that you plan to wear with the skirt. Trim the excess fabric from the inserts and stitch the skirt on the outside, carefully attaching the old fabric over the new insert.

Mark the hem with a yardstick or skirt marker. Most hems are 2″ to 3″ deep, depending on the weight of the fabric. Stitch the hem by hand or machine, depending on the look you prefer. Give your new skirt a good pressing before you hang it away. Wear and enjoy!

17
No-Sew Fashions

TAKE A PIECE of fabric, fold it, twist it, drape it, knot it—instant chic for practically pennies.

Scarves can become blouses, skirts, or sarongs. We turned a larger piece of hand-painted silk crêpe de chine into an evening dress; for a change, we also draped it as an evening skirt. Teamed with a simple black skirt, a $2 piece of black cotton became a two-piece party dress.

For these fashions, you'll want soft, supple fabrics that move well, because your garment's appearance depends on folding and draping, rather than on seam construction. Most of these garments have no more than two seams. Fabrics like knits, silks, velvets, wool, cashmere, and mohair solids or blends are good; heavy upholstery fabrics aren't, except for one pattern: the Cocoon Jacket/Coat. Since the designs depend so completely on the fabric you choose, you can make up two or three versions of some of your favorite designs, and they'll all look different. But remember: since the fabric is so essential in these designs, don't cut corners by buying cheap fabric. Even at $10 to $20 a yard, which we pay only for couture fabrics (on sale, of course), most designs take less than two yards of fabric—less than $40.

Do what most home sewers do: buy beautiful fabric cheaply at seasonal sales and put it away for future sewing projects. You'll soon learn how much fabric you need in 36", 45", 54", and 60" widths for simple tops, straight and full skirts, and wrap dresses. Sewers who plan ahead are never at a loss when they're suddenly faced with chunks of free time—like having to stay home with a sick child, or being snowed in. They just take out their fabric trunk or carton and get to work.

Here are some designs that should take you anywhere from ten minutes to less than three hours to make. They are all based on your measurements.

Strapless Tube Dress
Tube Skirt
Cocoon Jacket/Coat
Sarong Dress
Reversible Two-Color Sarong
      Dress

One-Shoulder Dress
Sandwich-Board Dress
Scarf Halter
Cowl-Neck Triangle Halter
Rectangular Top
Pareo Skirt

Not only are these designs fast and easy to make, but they also pack flat in no room at all. They're perfect for warm-weather weekends and vacations. With only two days' notice, you can whip up several outfits, pack them, and get away in a flash.

STRAPLESS TUBE DRESS

MATERIALS
2¾ yards 30″ to 36″ knit or woven fabric for full-length; 2¼ yards for
    street-length
1¼ yards ½″ elastic

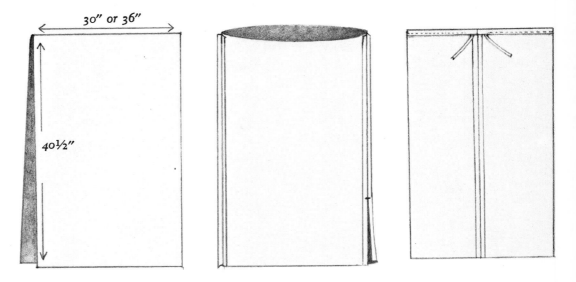

1. Fold fabric in half crosswise and cut along line.
2. Sew side seams, leaving slit, if desired, and hem slit.
3. At top of tube, fold over fabric and make casing for elastic, leaving approximately 2″ open.
4. Measure yourself snugly under your underarms. (You are allowing for the elastic's stretching.) Add 2″ to your measurement and cut elastic.
5. Run elastic through casing, overlap it 2″ for reinforcement, and sew securely. Close up casing.
6. Try on with appropriate shoes and make hem.

Since this is a very simple, dramatic design, you can make it look like half a dozen different dresses if you sew it in a basic fabric like black wool crêpe or silk jersey.

This is the ultimate design for busy travelers who have to change their evening looks and don't want to take five or six different outfits. In the shorter length, cotton jersey is a wonderfully versatile fabric for this style. It can go under a blazer or jacket for day and shine on its own at night.

TUBE SKIRT

MATERIALS

1¾ yards any width knit or woven fabric (Note: The wider the fabric, the fuller the finished skirt will be.)
1 yard ½″ elastic

THE STRAPLESS TUBE DRESS
TOP ROW:
Over a contrasting color cashmere sweater.
With a jeweled belt at waist or above bustline.

BOTTOM ROW:
Shortened by a fanny-wrapped hip scarf and a bandeau-knotted bustline.
With rhinestone clips to gather the sides.
Glamorized by a scarf knotted on one shoulder.

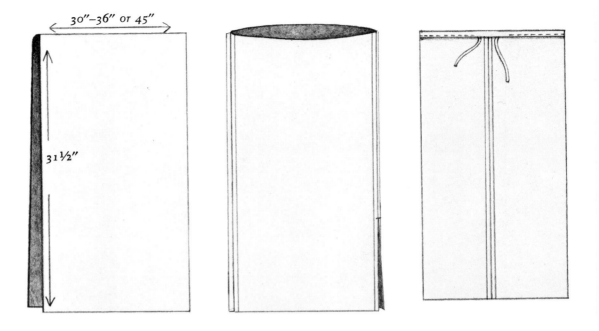

1. Fold fabric in half crosswise and cut along line.
2. Sew side seams, leaving slit, if desired, and hem slit.
3. At top of tube, fold over fabric and make casing for elastic, leaving approximately 2″ open.
4. Measure yourself snugly around your waist. (You are allowing for the elastic's stretching.) Add 2″ to your measurement and cut elastic.
5. Run elastic through casing, overlap it 2″ for reinforcement, and sew securely. Close up casing.
6. Try on with appropriate shoes and make hem.

For flounces and trimmings, see the skirt designs in the next chapter.

COCOON JACKET/COAT

MATERIALS

1½ yards 48″ or 50″ fabric for jacket, or a rectangle seamed, if
    necessary, to those dimensions; 2 yards 48″ or 50″ fabric for coat,
    or a rectangle in those dimensions
    Winter: coating-weight woolen
    Summer: cotton or silk or wool gauze
    Evening: brocade, velvet, or silk (hand-painted or printed)

TUBE SKIRT

1. Hem or fringe all sides.
2. Measure 20″ down and fold.
3. Stitch 5″ from open end on each side. These are your sleeves.
4. With the long side behind you, slip your arms into the sleeves and drape over your shoulders.

NOTE: If you're using patchwork quilts, antique rugs, or other precious antique fabrics and don't want to stitch the fabric together permanently, use snaps as a temporary closing that will not damage the fabric. Use three or four snaps on each side, as shown below, and match the size of the snaps to the weight of the fabric.

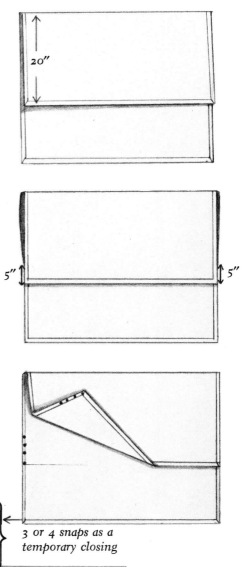

3 or 4 snaps as a temporary closing

COCOON JACKET

SARONG DRESS

MATERIALS

40" × 72" scarf or piece of fabric
Hem all sides of the fabric or fringe the edges, if desired. Wrap fabric
around your body, crisscrossing the two ends of the fabric and tying
them behind your neck, as illustrated in the diagram.

Or change the look by simply twisting the two ends of fabric, as if to
braid them together.

REVERSIBLE TWO-COLOR SARONG DRESS

This design can also be made with only one piece of fabric, but we love
the two-color reversible look and think you will, too.

MATERIALS

1½ yards each of two colors (two solids or a solid and a print) 45", 54",
or 60" fabric. Silk or a silklike fabric that drapes well is ideal for
this design.
4 safety pins for reversible design; 4 snaps or Velcro tape if dress is made
as one-piece

SARONG DRESS

1. To determine the length of your dress, center a measuring tape just above your breasts and measure over your abdomen down to the desired length. Add 2″ to this measurement for ease and 1″ more for finishing the seams and hem. The width is determined by the width of your fabric (44″, 45″, 54″, or 60″).

2. Cut both pieces of fabric to your desired length. Be sure that both pieces of fabric have exactly corresponding measurements.

3. Placing the right sides of the fabric together, as though you were making a huge pillowcase, pin the corners together and then all the seam lines, leaving an 8″ opening so that you cau turn the fabric right side out. Sew the fabrics together, leaving a ⅝″ seam allowance. Press the seams; then turn right side out.

4. Hand-sew the 8″ opening closed, making sure that your stitching doesn't show. Press the entire piece of doubled fabric. *That's all there is to it.*

To wear, wrap the fabric around you, starting at your left shoulder blade (A), across your back to your right shoulder blade (B) and around in front. Gather the remaining fabric, pulling up and twisting it tightly to form a strap which will go over your shoulder. Pin at points A, B, C, and D. You can use a decorative pin for C (and even D), or a safety pin, which should be positioned correctly so that it won't show. If you use snaps or Velcro tape, the sarong can't be reversible.

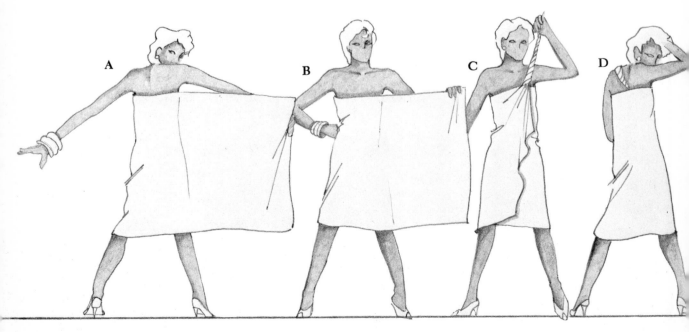

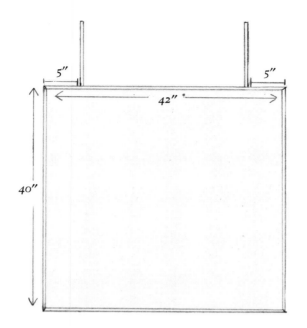

ONE-SHOULDER DRESS

MATERIALS

Length of fabric or scarf approximately 40″ × 42″
¼ yard 36″ wide fabric for straps or ribbon, cording, or braid
Velcro tape, 6 to 8 snaps, or buttons

1. Hem all sides of fabric, fringe it finely, or pipe the edges.
2. Make two straps approximately 15″ long and ½″ wide. They can be self-fabric, ribbon, cording, or braid.
3. Measure in 5″ from each top edge and tack down the straps, as shown.
4. Wrap the fabric around you and tie the straps over one shoulder. Mark where snaps or fastenings should be placed so the dress won't open.
5. Sew snaps, Velcro tape, or buttons in place.

SANDWICH-BOARD DRESS

MATERIALS

1¼ yards 54″ or 60″ fabric. Silk or a silklike fabric that drapes well is ideal for this design.
several snaps or Velcro tape

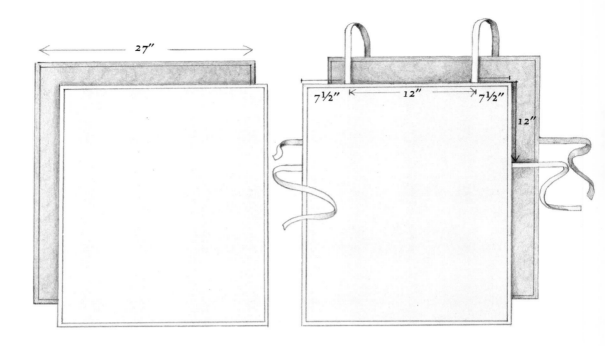

1. To determine the length of your dress, center a measuring tape just above your breasts and measure over your abdomen down to the desired length. Add 2″ to this measurement for ease and 1″ more for finishing the seams and hem. Cut two rectangles using this measurement for the length and 27″ for the width.
2. Hem all sides of both of the squares.
3. Make six straps ½″ wide and 15″ long. (Cut them 1″ wide to allow for hemming.)
4. Pin two of the shoulder straps to the square at the measurements indicated in the diagram and try the dress on. Alter the strap length and placement, if necessary. Tack in place, trim the ends if they're too long, and hem them.
5. Approximately 12″ down from the top of the dress, pin each of the four waist straps. Alter their placement, if necessary. Tack them in place and hem the ends.

PAGE 243: **SANDWICH-BOARD DRESS**
REVERSIBLE TWO-COLOR DRESS
ONE-SHOULDER DRESS

To wear, slip the dress over your head, like a sandwich board. Bring the front straps around and tie them in the back, over your slip or underwear.

Then place the back fabric down over the tied straps, carry the two back straps around to the front, and tie them over your tummy.

NOTE: You may want to put several snaps or Velcro down the sides of the dress to ensure that it stays closed.

SCARF HALTER

MATERIALS

Two 36″ square or triangular scarves, or fabric hemmed to those dimensions. Crêpe de chine is exquisite in this design.

Fold scarves in triangle, if necessary, and tie the ends together at center front, behind your neck and behind your back, as shown.

Presto! Your halter is tied and ready to wear.

COWL-NECK TRIANGLE HALTER

MATERIALS

Two triangles of fabric 25″ × 25″ × 40″, as shown. Silk knits and crêpe de chine are suggested.

SCARF HALTER

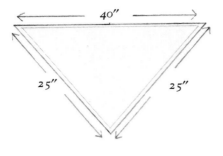

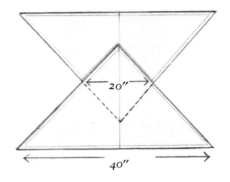

1. Hem the sides of the triangles.
2. Pin the triangles together, as shown, so that the two points are overlapping 20″ across.
3. Stitch the triangles together invisibly, or accentuate the overlap with machine stitching, for a designer detail.

To wear, knot the halter at your waist and behind your neck, as shown.

RECTANGULAR TOP

MATERIALS

⅓ yard of 45″ or 54″ fabric. This design works well in cotton as well as silk.

1. Measure your bustline, add 1½″ for hems, and cut a rectangle 10″ x this measurement. Hem all the edges.
2. With the remaining yardage, cut four straps 1″ × 15″. Hem the edges and attach to the corners of the rectangle, as shown.

To wear, wrap the rectangle around your body and tie, as illustrated.

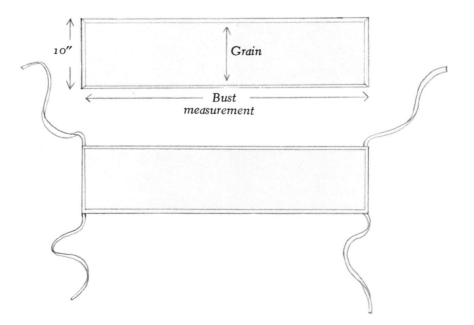

COWL-NECK TRIANGLE HALTER

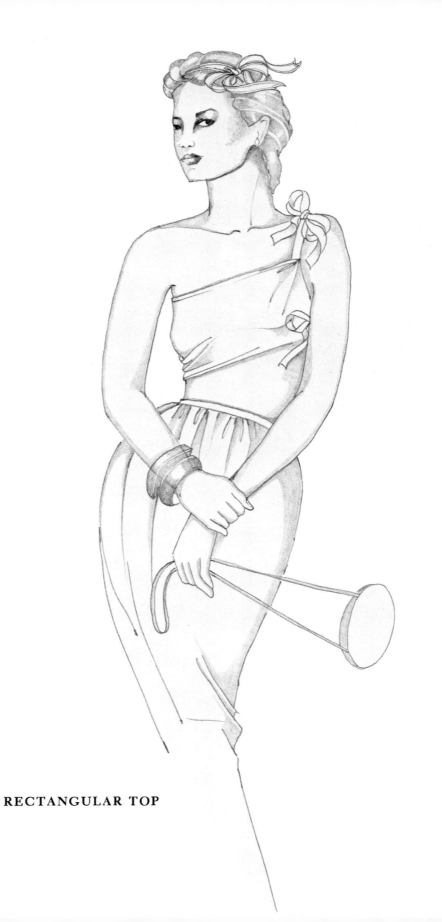

RECTANGULAR TOP

PAREO SKIRT COORDINATED
WITH RECTANGULAR TOP

PAREO SKIRT

MATERIALS

Sarong-style scarf or length of fabric 40″ × 72″. (If you prefer a shorter
skirt, the length can be 30″ to 36″, rather than 40″.)

1. Hem all sides of the fabric, or fringe the edges finely, if desired.

Hold one end of the scarf at your center front, as illustrated, and bring
the rest of the fabric around your body, swinging the long end around to the
front.

With your fingers, pleat the remaining fabric and tuck the gathered
area under. You may want to pin it with a brooch or decorative ornament,
as shown, as a safety measure to secure the fabric in place.

18
No-Pattern Designs

IF YOU'RE AN AVERAGE sewer, or if you've made up a couple of designs from the last chapter, these designs should be easy for you. They're only slightly more complicated than the designs in the preceding chapter. Most of them can be laid out directly on the fabric with tailor's chalk and a yardstick. A few need simple patterns that you can either draw directly onto the fabric or sketch quickly on brown paper (save your old grocery bags) and pin onto the fabric.

Most of these designs take less than five hours to make:

Evening Caftan
Kimono Evening Dress
Fringed Dirndl Skirt
Drawstring Pants
Ruffled Dirndl Skirt
Raglan-sleeved Peasant Blouse
Peasant Skirt
Matching Ruffled Shawl

EVENING CAFTAN

MATERIALS

3½ yards 48″, 54″, or 60″ lightweight, drapable fabric. Prints—especially hand-painted silks—are better than solids because of the visual impact of all the fabric in a caftan.

For Napped and One-Way Fabrics

1. Fold fabric crosswise and cut along fold.
2. Turn both pieces so that the motifs are going in the same direction, as shown.
3. At the top of each piece, find the midpoint and mark it with tailor's chalk. Measure 6″ in either direction and mark with tailor's chalk, as shown.
4. On the front piece, measure 2½″ down from the center mark and draw a curve connecting the chalk marks. Cut.
5. On the back piece, measure 1½″ down from the center mark and draw a curve connecting the chalk marks. Cut.
6. With right sides together, sew ⅝″ shoulder seam.
7. Hem the neck opening with a hand-rolled hem.
8. Measure down 10″ from shoulder seam and sew ⅝″ seam down to the bottom of the caftan on each side.
9. Try on caftan with appropriate shoes and shorten, if necessary, allowing 1″ for hand-rolled hem. Make hem.
10. Make hand-rolled hem on sleeves.

For Other Fabrics

1. Fold fabric crosswise and mark fold line with tailor's chalk. This is the shoulder line. Open fabric.
2. Find midpoint of fold line and mark with tailor's chalk. Measure 6″ in both directions and mark with tailor's chalk, as shown.
3. From midpoint, measure 1″ up (for back) and 2″ down (for front) and draw an oval opening connecting the chalk marks. Cut along chalk line.
4. Hem the neck opening with a hand-rolled hem.
5. Measure down 10″ from fold line and sew ⅝″ seam down to the bottom of the caftan on each side.
6. Try on caftan with appropriate shoes and shorten, if necessary, allowing 1″ for hand-rolled hem. Make hem.
7. Make hand-rolled hem on sleeves.

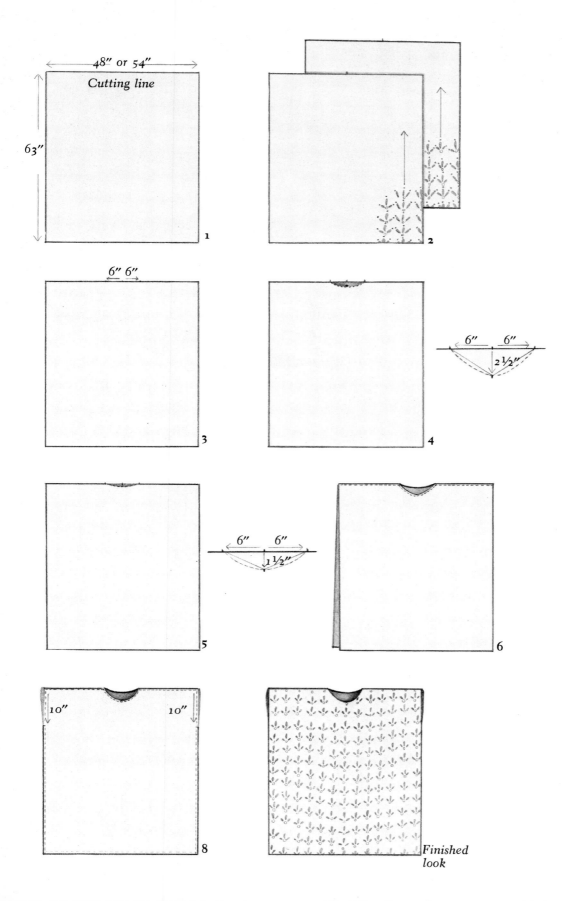

48" or 54"

Cutting line

63"

1

2

6" 6"

3

6" 6"

2½"

4

6" 6"

1½"

5

6

10"   10"

8

Finished
look

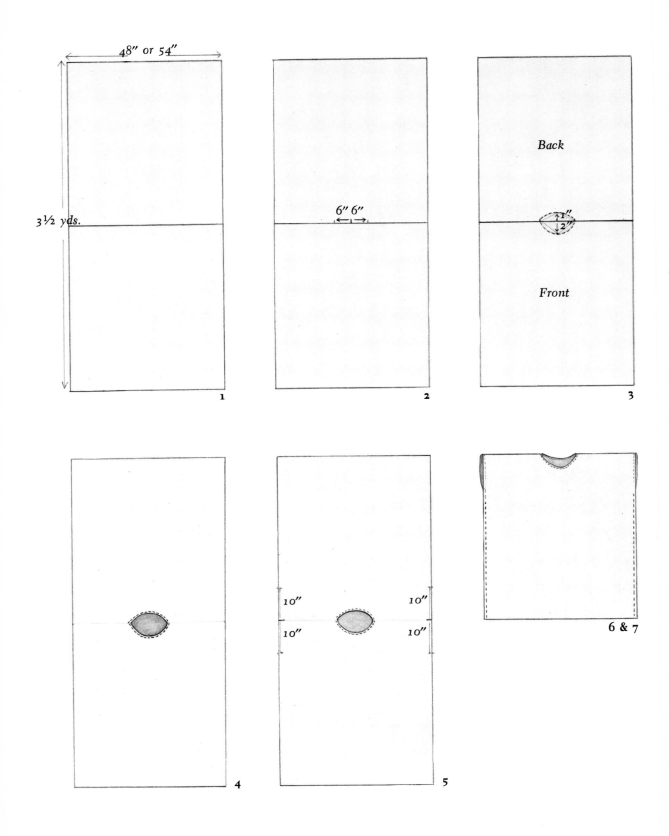

48″ or 54″

3½ yds.

6″ 6″

1″
2″

Back

Front

10″

10″

10″

10″

1

2

3

4

5

6 & 7

EVENING CAFTAN

KIMONO EVENING DRESS

MATERIALS

2½ yards 54″ or 60″ lightweight, drapable fabric. Prints—especially hand-painted silks—are better than solids because of the visual impact of all the fabric in this dress. Stripes are especially good because they emphasize the T-shaped lines of the dress.

1. Cut two rectangles 55″ long x 16″ wide and two rectangles 42″ long by 22″ wide, using the layout shown.
2. Taking the top rectangles, with right sides together, make ⅝″ shoulder seams by stitching in 21″ from the outside raw edge toward the center on each side, as shown in the diagram. To make the bateau neckline, turn under the raw edge of the 13″ neck opening, tack it down cleanly on the wrong side, and stitch invisibly.
3. Now stitch the other side of the rectangles 17″ from the outside raw edge toward the center on each side, as shown in the diagram, leaving a 21″ opening at the center for the skirt to be attached. To finish the sleeve, turn fabric under ⅛″ and press. Turn fabric under again ¼″ and hem. The top of the evening dress is complete.
4. Taking the skirt pieces, with right sides together, sew ½″ seams along the 42″ sides. Press open.
5. Pick up the top of the dress. Decide which is the top of your skirt. With right sides together, pin the skirt to the top, easing the material for a perfect match. Baste the garment and check. Stitch securely.
6. Try on with appropriate shoes and measure for hem. Make hem.

FRINGED DIRNDL SKIRT

MATERIALS

2 yards any 36″ to 45″ fabric. Wool challis makes beautiful cut fringes. Other lightweight and mediumweight woven wools can be raveled to make very fine fringes.

1 yard ½″ elastic

wooden or plastic beads, if desired

1. Fold fabric in half crosswise and cut along line.
2. Sew side seams.
3. At top of skirt, fold over fabric and make casing for elastic, leaving approximately 2″ open.

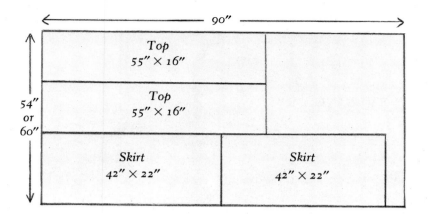

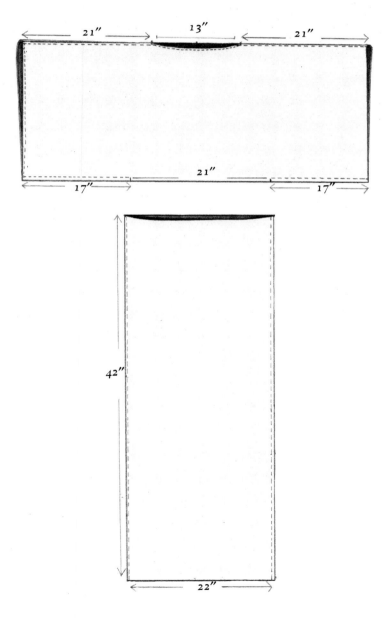

KIMONO EVENING DRESS

LEFT: *Fringed dirndl skirt*
RIGHT: *Drawstring pants*

4. Measure yourself snugly around your waist. (You are allowing for the elastic's stretching.) Add 2″ to your measurement and cut elastic.

5. Run elastic through casing, overlay it 2″ for reinforcement, and sew securely. Close up casing.

6. Try on and mark where you want finished hem length, including fringe. Cut at hem length and ravel or fringe to desired height: ½″ to 1″ fringed strips are a good width.

7. Knot wooden or plastic beads on the fringes, as desired.

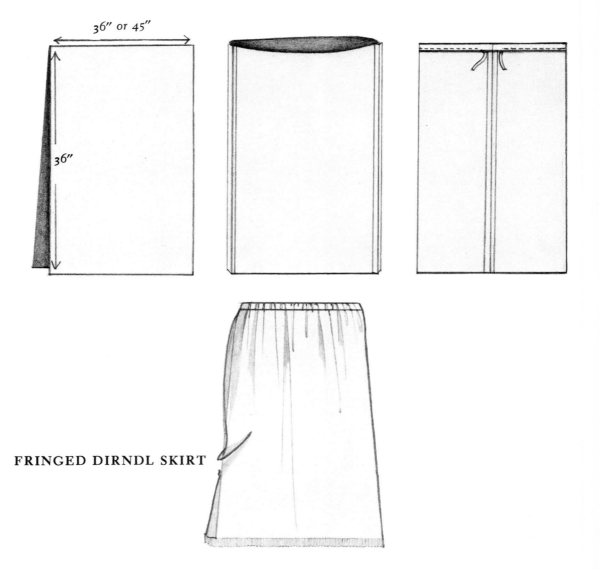

FRINGED DIRNDL SKIRT

DRAWSTRING PANTS

MATERIALS

2½ yards lightweight knitted or woven 30″ or 36″ fabric

1 yard cording or ½″ ribbon

1. If fabric has no nap or one-way pattern, fold fabric crosswise and begin. If fabric is napped or patterned, fold fabric crosswise, cut along fold, and place both pieces of fabric right sides together, with tops of the motifs corresponding to top (waist) of the pattern.
2. With tailor's chalk, draw two rectangles 14″ × 3½″, as shown. Then draw 1½″ diagonal lines from inner corners and draw curves, as shown.
3. Pin along insides of chalked lines and cut along chalked lines and along bottom fold line, if fabric has not already been cut.
4. Take one piece and fold it in half, with right sides together. Seam from A to B. Do the same with the other piece. These are the two legs.
5. For crotch seam, turn one pant leg right side out. Slip inside the remaining pant leg. Sew a U-shaped seam, as illustrated. Stitch again ¼″ away to reinforce seam.
6. At top of pants, fold over fabric and make casing for drawstring, turning fabric under ¼″ and pressing, then turning fabric under another ¾″ toward wrong side and stitching close to the edge, keeping a 2″ opening at the center front.
7. Try on pants with appropriate shoes. Make hem or make tight ankle cuffs of leftover fabric, from crotch cutout, as shown in knickers pattern in Chapter 16.

RUFFLED DIRNDL SKIRT

MATERIALS

2 yards any 36″ to 45″ lightweight, summery fabric

1 yard ½″ elastic

1. Cut four 4½″ crosswise strips. These will make the ruffle.
2. Fold remaining fabric in half crosswise and cut along line.
3. Sew side seams.
4. At top of skirt, fold over fabric and make casing for elastic, leaving approximately 2″ open.

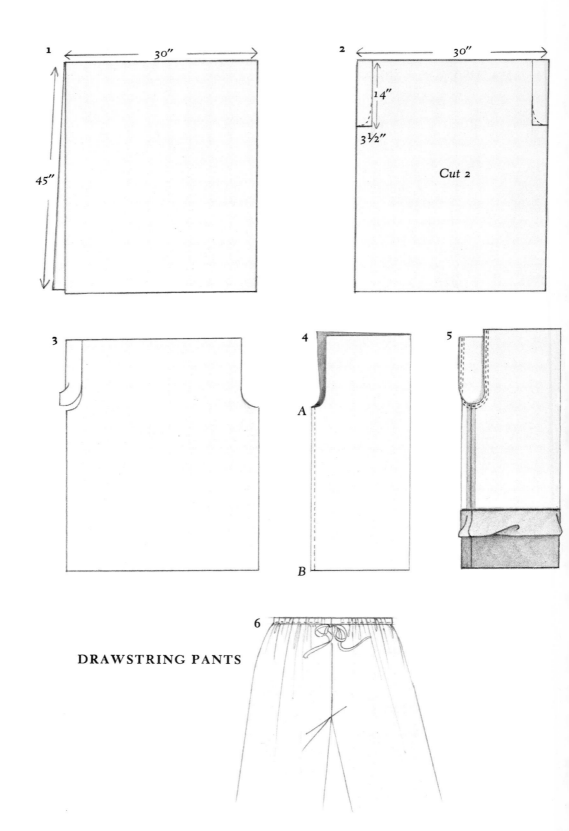

1 30"

45"

2 30"

14"

3½"

Cut 2

3

4
A

B

5

6

DRAWSTRING PANTS

5. Measure yourself snugly around your waist. (You are allowing for the elastic's stretching.) Add 2″ to your measurement and cut elastic.

6. Run elastic through casing, overlap it 2″ for reinforcement, and sew securely. Close up casing.

7. Seam ruffle strips end-to-end to form a circle and hem one long side. This will be the bottom of the skirt.

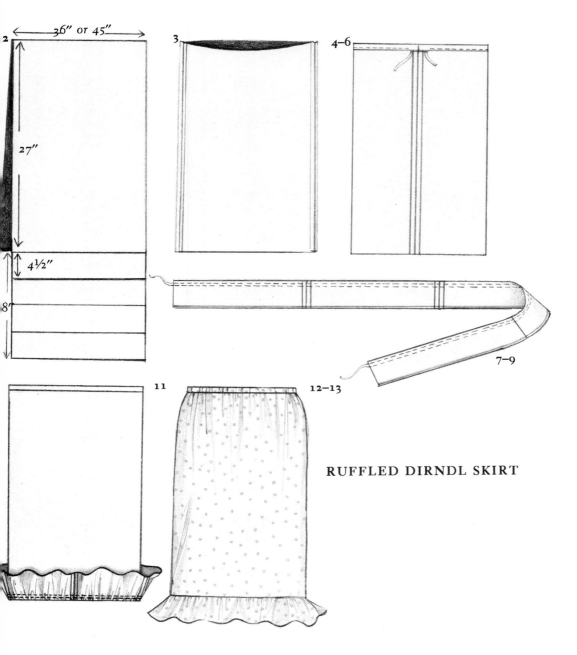

RUFFLED DIRNDL SKIRT

8. Try on skirt with appropriate shoes. With right sides of ruffle and skirt together, pin top of ruffle to bottom of skirt, with ½″ seam allowance. Check for finished length. If skirt is too long, cut it off at desired length, remembering to allow ½″ extra for the seam.

9. Sew two rows of basting stitches ¼″ apart, across the top of the ruffle.

10. Gather the ruffle.

11. Pin the ruffle in place, matching seams as shown in the diagram, and ease in the fullness, making sure that the gathering is balanced throughout. Pin and baste it.

Peasant blouse coordinated with the ruffled dirndl skirt

12. Now turn it to the right side and check to see that the ruffle falls correctly. Make sure that you haven't caught or bunched up bits of the ruffle or the skirt in your line of stitching.

13. Stitch permanently.

RAGLAN-SLEEVED PEASANT BLOUSE

MATERIALS

1½ yards 45″ knit or woven fabric
1 yard cording or ½″ ribbon
½ yard ¼″ elastic

1. Lay out the pattern pieces shown below with tailor's chalk, or make paper pattern first, if desired.
2. Placing right sides of front and back panels together, stitch side seams from point A to point B.
3. Fold each sleeve in half with right side inside and stitch from point C to point D.

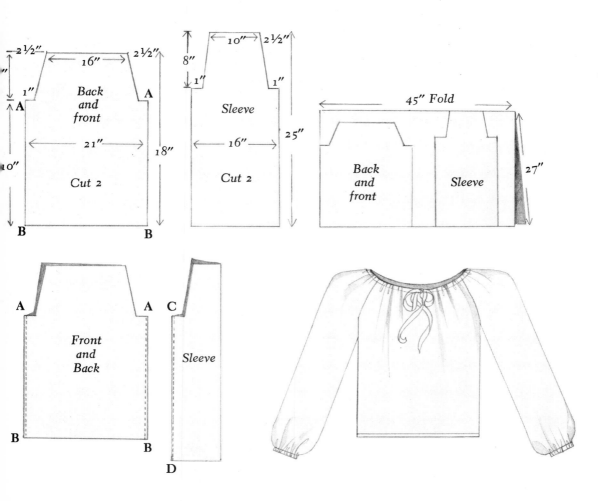

4. With right sides together, pin sleeves to arm openings, matching point C to point A at front and back of each opening. Sew.

5. To make a casing for the drawstring neck, fold fabric ⅛″ toward wrong side. Press. Fold in another ½″ and stitch close to edge, leaving ½″ opening in the center front. Run ribbon or cording through casing, tie, and flip bow over to outside of blouse.

6. Try on the blouse to check sleeve length. Pin to desired length and make a casing like the one for the blouse neckline. Insert elastic and fit comfortably on your wrist. Allow an additional 1″ for overlap. Stitch both ends of elastic together, overlapping 1″ for reinforcement, and completely close the wrist casings.

7. Check the blouse length, pin, and hem.

PEASANT SKIRT

MATERIALS

1½ yards 36″ fabric
1 yard cording or ½″ ribbon

1. Cut fabric as shown in diagram.

2. With right sides together, sew the top rectangles together along the 15″ side seams and press seams open.

3. Choose one side of this cylinder as your skirt top and mark the center front with tailor's chalk or a pin. Turn under ¼″ and press. Then turn under ¾″ toward wrong side and stitch close to the edge, leaving a 1″ opening at the center front.

4. Run cording or ribbon through the skirt casing and tie inside, flipping bow outside, if desired. (You can make an additional belt or sash from the remaining fabric.)

5. With right sides together, sew the ruffle pieces together along the 12″ side seams and press seams open.

6. Run two rows of basting stitches along top of ruffle and gather it to fit the bottom of skirt. Pin in place, matching side seams, and distribute ruffle fullness evenly. Stitch, trim, and press.

7. Try skirt on with appropriate shoes, pin, and hem.

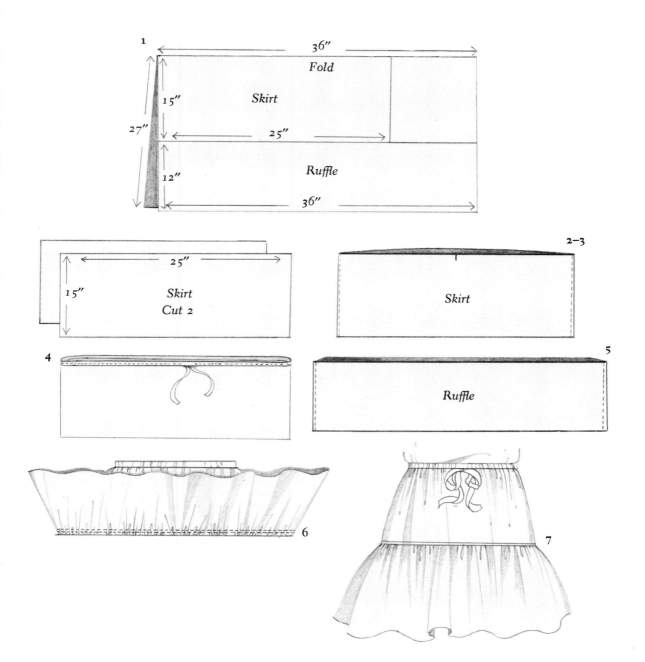

1

36"

Fold

Skirt

15"

27"

25"

12"

Ruffle

36"

2-3

25"

15"

Skirt
Cut 2

Skirt

4

5

Ruffle

6

7

PEASANT SKIRT AND RAGLAN-SLEEVED PEASANT BLOUSE

Ruffled shawl with appliqué ideas from Chapter 16

MATCHING RUFFLED SHAWL

MATERIALS

1½ yards of 36″ or 1¾ yards of 45″ fabric, to match your skirt

1. Cut fabric across to form a square 36″ × 36″ or 45″ × 45″.
2. Cut remaining 18″ strip into four 4½″ strips.
3. With right sides together, seam ruffle strips end to end to form a long strip. Hem the ends and one long side. This will be the bottom of the ruffle.

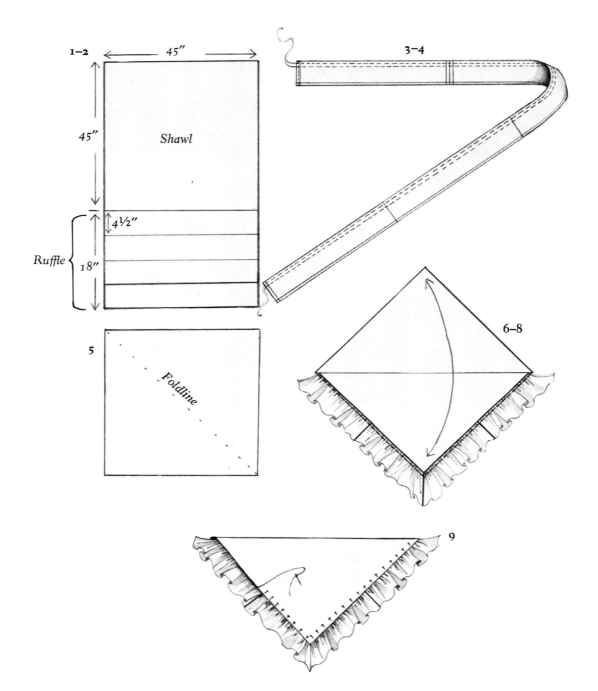

1–2

45″

45″

Shawl

4½″

Ruffle

18″

3–4

5

Foldline

6–8

9

4. Sew two rows of basting stitches ¼″ apart across the top of the ruffle.

5. Fold fabric square diagonally and baste across or press. Mark ⅝″ seam on shorter sides.

6. Gather ruffle, matching center seam of ruffle to triangular point (A) and side seams of ruffle to midpoints of sides (B) and (C), as shown in the diagram.

7. With right sides of ruffle and *one thickness of fabric triangle* together, stitch a ⅝″ seam, easing ruffle in at point A. (More expert sewers can miter this corner.)

8. Flip over the other half of fabric triangle, so that the ruffle seam is covered, pin, and hem or blindstitch along the pressed-in seam allowance.

A Biased Bibliography

AMONG ALL THE BOOKS on fashion and the shopping guides, our all-time favorite is Geneviève Dariaux's *Elegance: A Complete Guide for Every Woman Who Wants to Be Well and Properly Dressed on All Occasions.* (New York: Doubleday, 1964). While this book would undoubtedly have been much different if it had been written fifteen years later (and if Mme. Dariaux is still alive, we wish she'd update this marvelous book), *Elegance* is fascinating to read both as a social document by a witty Parisian couturiere and for all the information that is just as relevant today as it was when it was written. The material on fabrics, buttons, finishing, hems, linings, trimming, and zippers is especially well done and still useful.

Dover Publications produces an extensive list of needlework and crafts books, including nine books (at last count) of iron-on transfers alone! We also find Dover's cut-and-use stencil series wonderful sources of appliqué patterns. The design-motif series features ethnic designs from China, Japan, ancient and Pre-Columbian Mexico, Africa, Scandinavia, Russia, and Pennsylvania Dutch country. In addition, Dover's edition of Franz Meyer's classic work, *Handbook of Ornament,* is an excellent reference, but its illustrations are harder to transfer than those from the books mentioned earlier.

Looking Terrific by Emily Cho and Linda Grover (New York: Ballantine Books, 1978) is full of useful information, aided by helpful illustrations.

272

The authors' emphasis on the emotional language of clothes is especially valuable.

Elaine Louie's *Manhattan Clothes Shopping Guide* (New York: Collier Books/Macmillan, 1978). Most of the information—and prices—in this book are obsolete. However, its arrangement by neighborhoods—including places where a weary shopper can break for a snack or a meal—is very useful. We'd recommend this book more as background and as a "road map."

On the shopping-guide side, Jean Bird's excellent *Factory Outlet Shopping Guide* series is revised annually. Unfortunately, there are only six books in the series: New York/Long Island/Westchester, New England, Eastern Pennsylvania, New Jersey/Rockland County, Washington, D.C. area, and the Carolinas. We wish she'd publish guides for the Midwest and West Coast cities.

For people in the Greater Boston area, the "Recyclopedia" is a marvelous specialized directory of clothing exchanges and consignment and thrift shops in Boston and thirty-seven communities from Acton to Winchester (alphabetically). It even lists sports equipment exchanges. Send $1.00 to Compositions, Box 203, Sudbury, MA 01776.

That takes care of our recommendations. The big negative is the *Underground Shopper* series, more's the pity, since there are twelve metropolitan-area editions. But it's a drag to wade through the interminable cutesy puns and all that self-hype and brag to find the little real shopping information that exists. You're better off calling a friend who's a shopping fanatic and taking her advice.

The authors welcome comments, suggestions and ideas from their readers. You may contact them by writing to:

FASHION SURVIVAL MANUAL
Everest House, Publishers
33 West 60th Street
New York, N.Y. 10023

Index of Designers and Labels

Index of Stores and Sources